Clean Tech, Clean Profits

Understanding your sector & a switched-on international team & real passion & creative energy leading to bright ideas & sustainable solutions & making deals happen & that's Clean Tech with Bird & Bird

Bird & Bird is pleased to support this second edition of 'Clean Tech, Clean Profits'.

A truly international team, we provide a full range of contentious and non-contentious corporate, commercial and regulatory services. We are passionate about meeting the needs of our clients. Because our lawyers genuinely understand the dynamics, issues and opportunities in the clean tech sector, we're able to give clear, highly technical, practical advice to organisations at all stages of their development - from public to private sector and from start-ups to the board room of large multinationals seeking to establish and implement global strategies.

For further information please contact:

Michael Rudd

D: +44 (0)20 7415 6174
michael.rudd@twobirds.com

Matt Bonass

D: +44 (0)20 7415 6731
matt.bonass@twobirds.com

twobirds.com

Abu Dhabi & Beijing & Bratislava & Brussels & Budapest & Copenhagen & Dubai & Düsseldorf & Frankfurt & The Hague & Hamburg & Helsinki & Hong Kong & London & Lyon & Madrid & Milan & Munich & Paris & Prague & Rome & Shanghai & Singapore & Skanderborg & Stockholm & Warsaw

Corvus Consulting

Environmental Planning & Assessment Consultants

www.corvusconsulting.com

The Institute of Directors is *the* professional body for business leaders and we have been representing our members for over 100 years.

The IoD is an influential network reflecting the full spectrum of international business leadership from the largest public corporation to the smallest family firm.

With such a diverse membership, a broad portfolio of benefits and services has been carefully designed to ensure that you and your business receive the practical support you need to successfully fulfill your role as a Director.

IoD membership can add real value to your business. Benefits include free access to facilities offered in our prestigious premises in London, the UK and Europe, free business information and advice, professional development, training, conferences and publications to help you maximize your potential. This respected and influential organization works on your behalf, representing your concerns to government, and delivers you professional business support, wherever it is needed.

For more information about the IoD, visit www.iod.com.

Clean Tech, Clean Profits

Using effective innovation and sustainable business practices to win in the new low-carbon economy

Consultant editor: Adam Jolly

RECOMMENDED BY
INSTITUTE OF DIRECTORS

KoganPage

LONDON PHILADELPHIA NEW DELHI

This book has been endorsed by the Institute of Directors.

The endorsement is given to selected Kogan Page books which the IoD recognizes as being of specific interest to its members and providing them with up-to-date, informative and practical resources for creating business success. Kogan Page books endorsed by the IoD represent the most authoritative guidance available on a wide range of subjects including management, finance, marketing, training and HR.

The views expressed in this book are those of the author and are not necessarily the same as those of the Institute of Directors.

Publisher's note

Every possible effort has been made to ensure that the information contained in this book is accurate at the time of going to press, and the publishers and authors cannot accept responsibility for any errors or omissions, however caused. No responsibility for loss or damage occasioned to any person acting, or refraining from action, as a result of the material in this publication can be accepted by the editor, the publisher or any of the authors.

First published in Great Britain and the United States in 2010 by Kogan Page Limited
Second edition 2014

2nd Floor, 45 Gee Street	1518 Walnut Street, Suite 1100	4737/23 Ansari Road
London EC1V 3RS	Philadelphia PA 19102	Daryaganj
United Kingdom	USA	New Delhi 110002
www.koganpage.com		India

© Kogan Page, Adam Jolly and individual contributors, 2010, 2014

ISBN   978 0 7494 7041 8
E-ISBN   978 0 7494 7042 5

British Library Cataloguing-in-Publication Data

A CIP record for this book is available from the British Library.

Library of Congress Cataloging-in-Publication Data

CIP data is available.

Library of Congress Control Number: 2014016805

Typeset by Graphicraft Limited, Hong Kong
Printed and bound by CPI Group (UK) Ltd, Croydon, CR0 4YY

CONTENTS

List of figures **xv**
List of tables **xvi**
Foreword **xvii**

PART 1 The size of the challenge **1**

1.1 Towards the circular economy **3**

Ellen MacArthur, Ellen MacArthur Foundation

The limits of linear consumption 3
From linear to circular – accelerating a proven concept 4
An economic opportunity worth billions – charting the new
    territory 6
Substantial net material savings 6
The shift has begun – mainstreaming the circular economy 8
References 9

1.2 Energy innovation **11**

Rob Saunders, Technology Strategy Board

Competitive renewables 12
Smart energy 13
Innovate better 13

1.3 Zero Carbon Britain **15**

Paul Allen, Centre for Alternative Technology

Key actions 17

1.4 Powering change **21**

David Handley, RES

The advantage of on-site renewable generation 22
Renewable energy options for powering business 24

Effective energy management   26
Towards the future – a greener outlook for business?   26
Notes   27

PART 2 The potential for innovation   29

2.1 Low-carbon growth   31

Andy Eastlake, Low Carbon Vehicle Partnership

The policy backdrop   32
A 'virtuous circle'   33
Technology options and cost efficiency   34
Conclusion   34

2.2 Smarter buildings   37

Richard Solomon, KSR Architects

Integration is key   38
The business case   39
Create a great customer experience   39

2.3 Efficiency gains   41

Andrew Mitchell, CleanWeb Factory

Investment   41
Waste   43

2.4 Changes in corporate behaviour   45

Matt Bonass, Bird & Bird

Directors' duties under company law   46
Mandatory disclosure of environmental emissions   47
'Greening' the supply chain   49
Renewable energy generation   49
Opportunities for demand-side management and 'co-venturing'   50
Conclusion   50
Notes   52

2.5   Clean options on major projects   53

Tom Woollard and Nick Cottam, ERM

Project delays   53
Innovative project thinking   55
It's all in the planning   55
Design for the future   58
A clean tech blueprint   58

PART 3 How the market works   63

3.1   Funding future energy   65

Jeremy Biggs, Narec Capital

3.2   The value of measuring carbon   71

Melanie Eddis and Nick Cottam, ERM

CDP as a reporting driver   71
Third-party assurance   73
Material risks   74
Consumer behaviour   75

**3.3   Structuring techniques for demand-side management
solutions**   77

Michael Rudd, Bird & Bird

Demand-side management: an overview   78
Key issues   80
Conclusion   85
Notes   86

3.4   Responsibly sourced   87

Ian Nicholson, Responsible Solutions

Case studies of reputation   90
Early steps in the construction industry   91
Responsible sourcing in building services and M&E –
    the next steps   92
Conclusions   93

3.5   Energy system modelling   95

George Day, Energy Technologies Institute

What can modelling tell us?   96
The characteristics   96
Energy markets   97
The scale of investment   98

3.6   Intellectual property for clean tech   101

Nick Sutcliffe, Mewburn Ellis

Intellectual property protects innovation   101
Intellectual property is a business asset   102
Patents protect technical innovations   103
Any technical innovation may be patentable   103
Strategies for intellectual property   104
Management of intellectual property   104
Other people's intellectual property   105
Recycling old intellectual property   106

PART 4   Re-thinking energy   107

4.1   New demands on electricity   109

Mark Thompson and Martin Queen, Energy Innovation Centre

Innovation in energy generation   110
Innovation in energy use   111
Innovation in electricity distribution   113
Conclusion   115

4.2   Smart energy   117

Andrew Mitchell, CleanWeb Factory

The global context   118
Consumer behaviour   118
Super-useful information: who will win?   119
Notes   121

4.3 **The supergrid** 123

Godfrey Spickernell, Atlantic Supergrid

Harnessing the power of the planet 124
A European energy supergrid 124
The energy grids we have today 127
The emergence of a supergrid 128
What could the supergrid do for renewable energy? 132
Supergrid projects in development 134
Supergrid supporters and proponents 135
Bolstering existing AC grids 136
Laying an HVDC cable 140
Alternatives to the supergrid 141

4.4 **Prospects for self-generation** 143

Jodie Huggett, 4Eco

Self-consumption technologies 144
Clean efficiencies 146

4.5 **Pumped storage hydropower** 147

Catherine Anderson, AECOM

4.6 **Carbon capture and storage** 153

Judith Shapiro, Carbon Capture & Storage Association

Projects update 153
Costs and funding 155
Conclusion 156

PART 5 Renewable sources 157

5.1 **De-risking ocean energy** 159

Raymond Alcorn, Gordon Dalton, Mark Healy and Michael O'Connor, Beaufort Research

Current issues facing the industry – technical and non-technical barriers 161

De-risking the industry   163
Conclusion   164
Notes   166

5.2   Solar technology   169

Lee Sutton, 4Eco

The state of solar technology   169
The development of solar technology   170
Expectations for the future   172

5.3   Offshore renewable energy   173

Nick Medic, RenewableUK

Reference   178

5.4   Biomass   179

Professor Mike Bradley, The Wolfson Centre for Bulk Solids Handling Technology, University of Greenwich

What is it about biomass?   180
Examples of common handling problems with biomass   181
Why the problems?   181
Choosing the right solutions   182
Feedstock variability   182
Know your enemy   183
Note   184

PART 6   Environment   185

6.1   Water   187

Cees Buisman and Leon Korving, Wetsus

Energy from water   188
Control of antibiotic resistance and pharmaceuticals   193
Nutrient control and recovery   194
Conclusion   197

6.2   Current priorities for air pollution control   199

Professor Duncan Laxen, Air Quality Consultants Ltd

6.3   Resource efficiency   205

Katherine Adams, BRE

The problem   205
The opportunity   206
Design   206
New business models   207
Product collection and reuse   207
System changes   207
How can I adopt circular thinking?   208
What does the future hold?   208

PART 7 Transport   211

7.1   Powering tomorrow's electric vehicles   213

Dr Mark Crittenden and Huw Hampson-Jones, OXIS

Has the electric vehicle (EV) uptake gone to plan?   213
Some history first – the domination of the internal combustion
    engine   214
Introducing lithium sulfur   214
Safety   215
Performance   215
Clean tech   216
The first lithium sulfur vehicle   217
Mass-market adoption   217
EV battery improvements benefit other applications   218
Looking further ahead – lithium air   219

7.2   Transport design   221

Paul Priestman, Priestmangoode

7.3   Low-carbon mobility   227

Liam Lidstone, Energy Technologies Institute

Building blocks already in place   227
The chicken and the egg   228
What's best – charging at home or in the street?   228
A need to shift policy   229

7.4   LPG Autogas   231

Rob Shuttleworth, UKLPG

Note   234

Index   235
Index of advertisers   243

LIST OF FIGURES

FIGURE 2.5.1   Delayed extractive projects with CAPEX greater than $500m   54

FIGURE 2.5.2   At least 53% of projects have experienced a delay   56

FIGURE 2.5.3   Successful projects carefully consider all the alternatives   57

FIGURE 4.1.1   Electrical distribution network   114

FIGURE 4.3.1   Richard Buckminster Fuller's vision of a future Supergrid   123

FIGURE 4.3.2   Desertec's assessment of the area of the Sahara that would need to be covered with solar thermal generators to provide the world's electricity   125

FIGURE 4.3.3   Dr Gregor Czisch's European supergrid concept   126

FIGURE 4.3.4   Northern Europe – planned and existing connectors   129

FIGURE 4.3.5   High Voltage Direct Current HVDC links around the world   130

FIGURE 4.3.6   Wind energy links in various stages of planning and development   134

FIGURE 4.3.7   Energy links – a wider perspective   135

FIGURE 4.3.8   Plans for moving power south from Scotland, including two new HVDC marine cables, one on each coast ('bootstraps')   137

FIGURE 4.3.9   The American Wind Energy Association's proposed 765-kilovolt (kV) AC transmission grid   138

FIGURE 4.3.10   Standard break-even analysis between AC and DC   140

FIGURE 4.4.1   Effectively utilizing self-generated energy – immerSUN   145

FIGURE 5.5.1   A typical biomass process plant   180

FIGURE 5.5.2   Biomass feedstock   184

FIGURE 6.1.1   Schematic representation of the RED technology   191

FIGURE 6.1.2   Outline of the CO_2-technology for electricity generation from combustion off-gas   192

FIGURE 6.1.3   Fluidized UV LEDs with a TiO2 coating   194

FIGURE 7.2.1   Priestmangoode's *Moving Platforms* concept   223

FIGURE 7.2.2   High-speed trains of the future   225

LIST OF TABLES

TABLE 2.3.1 Energy consumption in the UK 2007–2012 44

TABLE 3.3.1 Demand-side management solutions and potential benefits 79

TABLE 4.1.1 Characteristics and spectrum of a range of energy sources 110

FOREWORD

Clean tech is set to revolutionize the assumptions on which organizations everywhere operate. Through a mixture of innovation and regulation, a future is being mapped out free of carbon and pollutants.

By 2020, we will have made a start in running our homes, workplaces and vehicles in smarter ways. By 2050, we should have reconfigured how we generate power, conserve water and manage waste.

For now, the gap between where we are and where we would like to be remains vast. To bridge it, we will require a whole series of innovations, a massive re-allocation of capital and the creation of new business models.

The consequences of these changes are certain to reach into all spheres of economic activity. Respond to clean tech in the right way and you could become one of the winners. Fail to grasp its implications as an underpinning technology and you could become one of the losers.

Drawing on a wide range of professional experience and commercial expertise, this book aims to give a practical guide to how organizations can re-think their operations, develop an innovative response, commercialize clean technologies and improve their efficiency.

Changes might happen as the result of a breakthrough or draw on a combination of existing techniques. They might be a flash of insight or a response to pressure from regulators and consumers. They might be an engineering design or a software programme. They could have global applications or be a quick fix.

Even once technically proven, the chances of any improvements reaching the market will still depend on whether the right economic signals are in place, whether capital can be raised and whether knowledge can be transferred.

This book is full of practical advice and concrete suggestions on how to capture the potential of clean tech and manage its implications. The IoD is grateful to all those who have given their knowledge and experience so freely.

Simon Walker, Director General,
Institute of Directors

PART ONE
The size of
the challenge

Towards the circular economy

Ellen MacArthur, sailor and founder of the Ellen MacArthur Foundation, explains why she is championing the case for a new economic model based on designing products for reuse throughout the industrial chain.

The last 150 years of industrial evolution have been dominated by a one-way or linear model of production and consumption in which goods are manufactured from raw materials, sold, used and then discarded as waste. In the face of sharp resource volatility increases across the global economy and proliferating signs of resource depletion, the call for a new economic model is getting louder.

The quest for a substantial improvement in resource performance across the economy has led businesses to explore ways to reuse products, their components or the materials within them thus preserving more of their precious material, energy and labour inputs. The time is right, many argue, to take this concept of a 'circular economy' one step further, to analyse its promise for businesses and economies and to prepare the ground for its wide adoption.

The limits of linear consumption

Throughout its evolution and diversification, our industrial economy has hardly moved beyond one fundamental characteristic established in the early days of industrialization: a linear model of resource consumption that follows a 'take-make-dispose' pattern. Companies harvest and extract materials, use them to manufacture a product, and sell it to a consumer – who then discards it when it no longer serves its purpose. Indeed, this is truer now than ever – in terms of volume, some 65 billion tonnes of raw materials entered the economic system in 2010, and this figure is expected to grow to about 82 billion tonnes in 2020.

Recently, many companies have also begun to notice that this linear system increases their exposure to risks, most notably higher resource prices and supply disruptions. More and more businesses feel squeezed between rising and less predictable prices in resource markets on one hand and high competition and stagnating demand for certain sectors on the other. The turn of the millennium marked the point when real prices of natural resources began to climb upwards, essentially erasing a century's worth of real price declines.

At the same time, price volatility levels for metals, food, and non-food agricultural output in the first decade of the 21st century were higher than in any single decade in the 20th century. If no action is taken, high prices and volatility will likely be here to stay if growth is robust, populations grow and urbanize, and resource extraction costs continue to rise. With 3 billion new middle-class consumers expected to enter the market by 2030, price signals may not be strong or extensive enough to turn the situation around fast enough to meet this growth requirement.

From linear to circular – accelerating a proven concept

A circular economy is an industrial system that is restorative or regenerative by intention and design. It replaces the 'end-of-life' concept with restoration, shifts towards the use of renewable energy, eliminates the use of toxic chemicals, which impair reuse and return to the biosphere, and aims for the elimination of waste through the superior design of materials, products, systems, and, within this, business models.

Such an economy is based on a few simple principles. First, at its core, a circular economy aims to 'design out' waste. 'Waste' does not exist – products are designed and optimized for a cycle of disassembly and reuse. These tight component and product cycles define the circular economy. They set it apart from disposal and even recycling where large amounts of embedded energy and labour are lost, with most current recycled materials being the most we can get out from products which are not designed for materials recovery. At minimum, with a circular economy products are designed for disassembly and recovery of basic materials – even at the very end of product life some value can be recovered. Second, circularity introduces a strict differentiation between consumable and durable components of a product. Unlike today, consumables in the circular economy are largely made of biological ingredients or 'nutrients' that are at least non-toxic and possibly even beneficial, and can be safely returned to the biosphere – directly or in a cascade of consecutive uses. Durables such as engines or computers, on the other hand, are made of technical nutrients unsuitable for the biosphere, like metals and most plastics. These should be designed from the start for reuse, and products subject to rapid technological advances are designed for upgrade. Third, the energy required to fuel this cycle should be renewable, again to decrease resource dependence and increase system resilience (eg to oil shocks).

For technical materials, the circular economy largely replaces the concept of a consumer with that of a user. This calls for a new contract between businesses and their customers based on product performance. Unlike in today's 'buy-and-consume' economy, durable products are leased, rented, or shared wherever possible. If they are sold, there are incentives or agreements in place to ensure the return and thereafter the reuse of the product or its components and materials at the end of its period of primary use.

These principles all drive four clear-cut sources of value creation that offer arbitrage opportunities in comparison with linear product design and materials usage:

- The *power of the inner circle* refers to minimizing comparative material usage vis-à-vis the linear production system. The tighter the circle, ie, the less a product has to be changed in reuse, refurbishment and remanufacturing and the faster it returns to use, the higher the potential savings on the shares of material, labour, energy and capital embedded in the product and on the associated rucksack of externalities – such as greenhouse gas (GHG) emissions, water, toxicity.

- The *power of circling longer* refers to maximizing the number of consecutive cycles (be it reuse, remanufacturing, or the cycling of materials) and/or the time in each cycle.

- The *power of cascaded use* refers to diversifying reuse across the value chain, substituting for an inflow of virgin materials into the economy.

- The *power of pure inputs* lies in the fact that uncontaminated material streams increase collection and redistribution efficiency while maintaining quality, particularly of technical materials, which, in turn, extends product longevity and thus increases material productivity.

These four ways to increase material productivity are not merely one-off effects that will dent resource demand for a short period of time during the initial phase of introduction of these circular setups. Their lasting power lies in changing the run rate of required material intake.

An economic opportunity worth billions – charting the new territory

Eliminating waste from the industrial chain by reusing materials to the maximum extent possible promises production cost savings and less resource dependence. However the benefits of a circular economy are not merely operational but strategic, not just for industry but also for customers, and serve as sources of both efficiency and innovation.

Economies will benefit from substantial net material savings, mitigation of volatility and supply risks, drivers for innovation and job creation, improved land productivity and soil health and long-term resilience of the economy.

Substantial net material savings

Based on detailed product-level modelling, the first report produced by the Ellen MacArthur Foundation with analysis by McKinsey & Company estimates that, in the medium-lived complex products industries, the circular economy represents a net material cost saving opportunity of US $340–380 billion per annum at EU level for a 'transition scenario' and US $520–630 billion per annum for an 'advanced scenario', in both cases the net value of the materials used in reverse-cycle activities. The latter would equate to 19–23 per cent of current total input costs or a recurrent 3–3.9 per cent of 2010 EU GDP. Benefits in the advanced scenario are highest in the automotive sector (US $170–200 billion per annum), followed by machinery and equipment.

For fast-moving consumer goods, the full value of circular opportunities, globally, could be as much as US $ 700 billion per annum in material savings or a recurring 1.1 per cent of 2010 GDP, all net of materials used in the reverse-cycle processes. Those materials savings would represent about 20 per cent of the materials input costs incurred by the consumer goods industry.

Mitigation of price volatility and supply risks

The resulting net material savings would result in a shift down the cost curve for various raw materials. For steel the global net material savings could add up to more than 100 million tonnes of iron ore in 2025 if applied to a sizeable part of the material flows (ie, in the steel-intensive automotive, machining and other transport sectors, which account for about 40 per cent of demand).

Innovation

The aspiration to replace one-way products with goods that are 'circular by design' and create reverse logistics networks and other systems to support the circular economy is a powerful spur to new ideas.

Job creation potential

A circular economy might bring greater local employment, especially in entry-level and semi-skilled jobs, which would address a serious issue facing the economies of developed countries. The total prize is just the beginning of a much bigger set of transformative value-creation plays as the world scales up the new circular technologies and business models. In a world of 9 or 10 billion consumers with fierce competition for resources, market forces are likely to favour those models that best combine specialized knowledge and cross-sector collaboration to create the most value-per-unit of resource over those models that simply rely on ever more resource extraction and throughput.

Land productivity and soil health

Land degradation costs an estimated US $40 billion annually worldwide, without taking into account the hidden costs of increased fertilizer use, loss of biodiversity and loss of unique landscapes. Higher land productivity, less waste in the food value chain and the return of nutrients to the soil will enhance the value of land and soil as assets. The circular economy, by moving much more biological material through the anaerobic digestion or composting process and back into the soil, will reduce the need for replenishment with additional nutrients.

Lasting benefits for a more resilient economy

Importantly, any increase in material productivity is likely to have a positive impact on economic development beyond the effects of circularity on specific sectors. Circularity as a 'rethinking device' has proved to be a powerful new frame, capable of sparking creative solutions and stimulating innovation. A circular economy would shift the economic balance away from energy-intensive materials and primary extraction. It would create a new sector dedicated to reverse cycle activities for reuse, refurbishing, remanufacturing, or recycling on the technical side, and anaerobic digestion, composting, cascading on the biological side.

The shift has begun – mainstreaming the circular economy

Why now? Our economy currently seems locked into a system in which everything from production economics and contracts to regulation and the way people behave favours the linear model of production and consumption. However, this lock-in is weakening under the pressure of several powerful disruptive trends: resource scarcity and tighter environmental standards are here to stay, information technology is now so advanced that it can trace materials anywhere in the supply chain and finally, we are in the midst of a pervasive shift in consumer behaviour – a new generation of consumers seems prepared to prefer access over ownership, especially when they are lower-cost, better product options. The time is right for a regenerative model, capable of providing long-term benefits, to be taken up to scale.

Ellen MacArthur made yachting history in 2005, when she became the fastest solo sailor to circumnavigate the globe. Having become acutely aware of the finite nature of the resources our linear economy relies upon, she stepped away from professional sailing to launch the Ellen MacArthur Foundation in 2010, which works with education and business to accelerate the transition to a regenerative circular economy. Ellen MacArthur sits on the European Commission's Resource Efficiency Platform, and her Foundation has published two seminal macro-economic reports featuring analysis by McKinsey, which have received accolades at the World Economic Forum in Davos. Dame Ellen regularly interacts with various European governments and institutions such as the Organization for Economic Co-operation and Development (OECD), and received the French Legion of Honour from President Nicolas Sarkozy, three years after having been knighted by Queen Elizabeth.

For more information please visit: **www.ellenmacarthurfoundation.org**.

References

McKinsey & Company (2012) Economic and business rationale for an accelerated transition, *Towards the Circular Economy*, 1

McKinsey & Company (2013) Opportunities for the consumer goods sector, *Towards the Circular Economy*, 2

Energy innovation

Rob Saunders, head of energy at the UK Innovation Agency,
the Technology Strategy Board, comments on how innovation can benefit
businesses while bringing ambitious targets in policy within reach.

The potential for innovation in energy is enormous. New markets worth billions will open up to those who find a way round the triple challenge of making energy more secure, more affordable and lower in carbon.

When you look at the targets for how much we have to improve, it can look daunting, but technology is giving us the capacity to re-think the rules and move beyond what we thought possible until quite recently. While some more traditional areas of energy are slower paced, the speed of change in other technology areas is phenomenal. For example the roll-out of smart meters planned for 2018; will these boxes on our walls be obsolete by the time they are implemented? Already we see apps emerging to monitor energy usage. By 2018 the use of digital, sensing and communications technologies in energy will mean we will probably be monitoring the flows of energy in and out of our houses on our mobiles, or some smart system will be automatically regulating our interactions with the energy system for us, minimizing our costs but making sure we have energy when we need it.

As well as saving us an expensive fit-out, such a leapfrog in technology could create a more complete picture of how energy is being consumed across whole neighbourhoods and the nation, opening up the scope for further efficiencies. No wonder major players like Google are building up their presence around these kinds of technologies.

Right across our energy industries, niches are being found that could scale up into products in everyday use. The work around hydrogen as a flexible fuel and storage medium, for instance, is starting to look really interesting and innovative ventures are starting to make an international impact. In energy systems, we are launching a 'catapult' centre to bring together the UK's innovative capabilities to help business pursue a market for energy networks optimization that could be worth £1.6 trillion by 2050.

On the supply side, as yet we can only take a portfolio approach to developing new energy technologies. No one knows for sure how they will play out in the market with more traditional sources.

It will only be by the mid-2020s that we are likely to see different low carbon supply technologies competing openly. Until then, it makes sense to pursue a number of different technologies and make sure that we innovate well.

Competitive renewables

As a guide to the future, one benchmark has just been set by the government for where it sees the future price of electricity. Its strike price for developing a new nuclear station with EDF at Hinkley was set at £93 per megawatt-hour (MWh) so the obvious challenge for renewables is to find a pathway to below this level of cost by the mid-2020s. Estimates put offshore wind at around £130–£140 per megawatt-hour. Through a taskforce for cutting costs, the industry is targeting a drop to about £100 per megawatt-hour by 2020.

Manufacturing scale-up will help, but a significant load will lie on innovation, such as bigger turbines, novel foundations and operation and maintenance. As offshore wind moves further out to sea and into deeper waters, questions will be asked about how best to support turbines and secure them to the seabed, as well as about how to maintain performance in often severe weather conditions.

Power from tides and waves remains less developed. Unlike offshore wind, no one is yet installing multiple turbines. Technology is still being prototyped and tested, so we are still looking for proof that technologies can run on an industrial scale.

Solar is gaining impetus and a number of large farms are being built across southern England. Their underlying technology might largely be built elsewhere, but we are now entering a new cycle of innovation, looking at how to make organic and flexible photovoltaics, as well as how to integrate them into building materials.

Clearly, fossil fuels will continue to play a critical role for years to come, giving us the capacity to meet surges in demand and guard against interruptions in supply. Their role will be maintained well into the future, if techniques for capturing and storing carbon emissions (Carbon capture and storage – CCS) can be brought into use. After a long hiatus, the Department of Energy and Climate Change (DECC)'s recent £1 billion competition to demonstrate two pilot schemes shows signs of getting CCS moving again in the UK.

Smart energy

Equally significant gains could result if we rethink our systems for taking power to the user. At the moment, we have an infrastructure that was built many years ago to meet demand by turning supply up or down. Power only ever flowed one way and storage was limited.

We now want a system that can cope with variations in supply and demand and in which energy can flow back from distributed generation as well as forward. At the same time, we are anticipating much heavier use of electricity at home in powering up electric vehicles and using heat pumps. It adds up to a major transformation.

The reality is that we will have to modify our infrastructure rather than build it again. The goal where possible will be to take the load off the main grid and make users more self-dependent.

The search for ways to optimize the system will lead to significant opportunities in controls, software and hardware, as well as techniques for modelling the system, in which the UK has strong capabilities.

Innovate better

In the UK, we have a good record for disruptive ideas and entrepreneurial solutions. We are less good at joining up the whole system to support technologies all the way into the market.

In energy, innovative ventures often find it hard to open a dialogue with the major players. One of our priorities at the Technology Strategy Board is to encourage collaboration across the supply chain, bringing together all those with a stake in finding a solution. Our catapult centres in areas such as off-shore renewable energy, future cities and energy systems, are designed as hubs for innovation around which knowledge, talent and capital can gather.

For those looking to access funding, our new energy catalyst can fund sizable projects up to the value of £250,000 to help you prove technical feasibility at its early stage; up to £3 million to develop your technology at the mid-stage of development; and up to £10 million to validate that technology at a late stage before you move into production. In addition, technology-specific competitions continue to run where we hope to stimulate new activity or partnerships that are not emerging naturally, or as particular challenges arise. In the Spring of 2014, for instance, bids were invited to revive the capabilities of the supply chain in Britain's nuclear industries.

Our goal is to make sure that the right technologies come through at the right time. By linking up innovation with the broader regulatory and commercial context, we can start to find ways of producing cleaner energy competitively.

For more information please visit: **www.innovateuk.org/energy**.

Zero Carbon Britain

Smart, conscious, integrated. **Paul Allen** at the Centre for Alternative Technology sets out a scenario for rethinking our future.

People all over the world are now experiencing first-hand the human and economic costs of our changing climate. Many are beginning to wonder just how much worse it could get. The science is clear – the public know this is a very serious problem, and politicians from all parties are being told to put away the political football and step up to the mark. There is also an increasing recognition amongst Earth Systems scientists that current UK greenhouse gas emissions targets, though ambitious in comparison to some of our international contemporaries, do not offer substantial enough reductions to provide a good chance of avoiding what is now considered extremely dangerous climate change. Neither do they adhere to what might be termed the UK's 'fair share' of the remaining global carbon budget that it is safe to burn. The most recent science demands an urgency that is not yet reflected in the mainstream approach.

The challenges of the 21st century cannot be solved with a 20th-century mindset; they require a smart, conscious and integrated approach. We need tougher decarbonization targets – and we must deliver them in a way that directly synergizes with the adaptation required to increase our resilience to the changes already in the system. Unfortunately such a transition remains beyond the boundaries of what is currently 'politically thinkable' and so becomes as much a challenge for our democracy and culture as it is for our technology. Like many other countries, the UK finds itself in a catch-22 situation in which business, government and civil society are all looking to each other for leadership on climate. We, as a society, have so far been hesitant to act, as government rhetoric does not reflect the scale of the threat outlined by science. Government focuses on the electoral horizon, not daring to take bolder action out of concern that they lack corporate and social mandate, and may lose votes or media backing. Business, on the other hand, looks to government for certainty that policy will offer long-term stability for investment in decarbonization and developing low carbon products, jobs and skills. These interdependencies have prevented action at the scale and speed necessary to tackle climate change. Despite urgent new evidence, far too little progress has been made.

The overwhelming scientific consensus is clearly pointing the way forward – but our vested interests are dragging us in almost the opposite direction. As more and more of us piece together this alarming big picture, it becomes one of the deepest and most pervasive sources of anxiety in our time. We see this, we know this, we realize the consequences, but society has created taboos against the public expression of such emotion and anguish. We simply put it away in that locker, just out of our conscious thought, where smokers keep the knowledge about lung cancer while they get on with the immediate challenges of the day. Yet if we are unable to imagine a positive, climate safe future, how can we create it?

What would it be like if we actually rose to the climate challenge? Is there a scenario that integrates cutting-edge knowledge and experience from a wide range of disciplines to model how Britain can reduce its greenhouse gas emissions rapidly to net zero over a couple of decades? What gains might we also make in our diet, health and wellbeing?

Our research shows that we can totally decarbonize the UK using existing technologies. By making changes to our buildings, transport systems and behaviour, and by investing in a variety of renewable energy generation technologies suited to the UK, we can provide a reliable zero carbon energy supply without significant impacts on quality of life. Smart demand management, plus the intelligent use of surplus electricity in combination with biomass to create carbon-neutral synthetic gas and liquid fuels, mean that we could meet our entire energy demand without imports, and also provide for some transport and industrial processes that cannot run on electricity.

In this scenario, growing second-generation energy crops on UK land provides all the required biomass – none is imported. All our cropland is still used for food production, and we produce the vast majority of the food required to provide for the UK population on home soil. Changing what we eat (mainly through a significant reduction in meat and dairy products, coupled with increases in various other food sources) means we eat a more healthy and better balanced diet than we do today, while our agricultural system emits fewer greenhouse gases and uses less land both at home and abroad, thus decreasing the environmental impact of our food production globally.

Key actions

The key areas of action are powering down energy demand, powering up renewable energy and changes in land use. If the actions suggested in the report were taken up, our greenhouse gas (GHG) emissions would decrease from 652 MtCO2e to just 38 MtCO2e – a reduction of 94 per cent. Our remaining effect on climate change would be equivalent to 45 MtCO2e in total.

The largest contribution to the reduction in GHG emissions is due to changes in our energy system – demand has been reduced by about 60 per cent from 1,750 terawatt-hours (TWh) today to 665 terawatt-hours through a number of energy saving measures and the amount we travel and move goods. We would produce 1,160 terawatt-hours of clean energy to supply our needs, covering losses in the system, requirements for synthetic gas and liquid fuels and back up to balance supply and demand.

With regard to land use – emissions from agriculture have decreased substantially – by roughly 73 per cent. This is largely due to changes in our diet, including significant decreases in the amount of meat and dairy we eat, plus changes in management practices. In total, about 17 per cent of our land is used to produce energy in some way, either fuel for transport and industry or as back up for our electricity system. Over half of our agricultural land is still dedicated to livestock (sheep and cows) in some way – either grazing grassland or growing feed. Another key change to our landscape is a doubling of the area of forest.

All together, these changes to the way we use land, the increased area of forest, the restoration of 50 per cent of our peat lands, and the use of more plant-based products made mainly from harvest wood, allow us to capture about 45 MtCO2e every year.

This balances out the emissions left in our scenario, meaning that we capture the amount of GHGs equivalent to our remaining impact every year – we are net zero carbon.

We balance out some residual greenhouse gas emissions that cannot currently be eliminated from non-energy processes (industry, waste and agriculture) by using safe, sustainable and reliable natural methods of capturing carbon. By restoring important habitats such as peat land, and by substantially expanding forested areas, we not only capture carbon but also provide wood products for buildings and infrastructure, rich environments for biodiversity and more natural spaces for all of us to enjoy. An initial analysis shows that these actions can also help us adapt to expected changes in climate while increasing our resilience to unexpected changes; improve upon a number of other significant environmental challenges aside from climate change; create over a million jobs; and positively impact on our economy and on the health and wellbeing of individuals and society.

Rather than residing precariously at the end of the peaking pipeline of polluting fossil fuel imports, Britain can head an indigenous renewable energy supply chain powering a lean, re-localized economy. Fields, forests, islands, rivers, coastlines, barns or buildings hold potential to become both energy- and revenue-generators, with different technologies appropriate to every scale or location. Britain can stay ahead of events through creating a new kind of economy: stable in the long term, locally resilient but still active in a global context, rich in quality jobs, with a strong sense of purpose and reliant on indigenous, inexhaustible energy.

By their very nature these renewable reserves will not peak. In fact, as the technology matures and becomes economic in a wider range of applications, the available reserves actually increase. *Zero Carbon Britain: Rethinking the future* provides a positive and technically feasible future scenario that explores how we can achieve what is necessary, closing the gap between current 'politics as usual' and 'what is physically necessary to address climate change'. This kind of transition is the cornerstone of a new economic approach that will move society onwards. By learning the hard economic lessons of the past few decades we can refocus the ingenuity of the finance sector on the actual challenges at hand. Once we have eyes to perceive our world differently, we will be able to act differently. A cultural shift will have been catalysed, with legal and administrative frameworks following suit to implement the physical reforms – and we know from history that such cultural shifts ripple out quite quickly.

But the window of opportunity is closing – many people are experiencing climate change first hand, and now is the time to act. The credit crunch has shown us the consequences of not reacting ahead of events. If we ignore the warnings and wait until the climate/energy crunch is really upon us before becoming serious about scaling up the solutions, in the ensuing chaos and dislocation we may struggle to muster the resources required to adapt. Such a rapid decarbonization will be the biggest undertaking we have made in generations, so it will require a great many to commit to the challenge, but in doing so we will find a sense of collective purpose we have been craving for a very long time.

Paul Allen, BEng (Hons), FRSA holds an honours degree in electronic and electrical engineering from Liverpool University. As External Relations Officer at the Centre for Alternative Technology, he heads the Zero Carbon Britain strategy programme, liaising with key policy makers in government, business and the public sector to disseminate the findings of the programme's evidence-based scenario work. The full report is available, free to download, via **www.cat.org.uk**.

Further information is available from Paul Allen
(tel: 01654 705958; e-mail: **paul.allen@cat.org.uk**;
websites: **www.cat.org.uk**; **www.zerocarbonbritain.com**).

Powering change

A greener outlook is good for business, says **David Handley** at Renewable Energy Systems (RES).

With 2013 recently acknowledged as being tied for the fourth-warmest year on record around the world,[1] governments, businesses and civil societies are coming under increasing pressure to take steps to address climate change.

We are also facing an unprecedented increase in demand for energy. According to the World Energy Council, demand for energy across the globe is expected to increase anywhere between 27 and 61 per cent by the year 2050.[2] Coupled with the worrying expected impacts of warming above 2 degrees centigrade, there isn't a better time to reconsider our personal and professional contributions to the low carbon transition.

One increasingly popular method for business to lower its carbon footprint is by generating its own energy via green sources. Latest estimates suggest that in the UK, on-site renewable energy generation could meet 14 per cent of energy demand by 2030, saving UK businesses approximately £33 billion between 2010 and 2030.[3]

In recent months, we have seen a diverse selection of companies from various industries using renewable energy to power their business. Generation projects at numerous high-profile companies have ignited media interest, including: BMW, Honda, BSkyB, Wal-Mart, Facebook and Apple. These companies have recognized the added value to their brand, their bottom line and their risk exposure as a result of including renewable energy in their energy portfolios.

The advantage of on-site renewable generation

What are the advantages of using on-site renewables to power growth? Increasingly, the concept of an 'energy trilemma' is emerging in conversations throughout industry and politics. This new buzzword refers to the challenge of reaching a balance between three key factors: energy sustainability, cost and security.

Individually, these three factors can all be improved through use of on-site generation. Whilst the sustainability aspects may initially be more apparent, renewable energy also provides cost benefits and increased energy security.

On-site generation is more sustainable than relying on the central grid. Leading companies have specific objectives to take their energy supply in-house through renewable energy targets. By accessing their on-site renewable energy resource, they are able to promote their sustainability credentials and build upon their reputation for being environmentally friendly. This in turn has an important effect on brand value.

The financial advantages of a renewable investment can vary, and are based on a number of factors. Local resource, market regulations, retail electricity prices and government support all play an important role in assessing potential payback. Depending on how these factors interplay, we have seen projects with a payback period of less than five years. It is more common for projects to have a 5- to 10-year payback, and in some cases 10-plus years. However, projects with a longer payback period still generate a healthy return.

On-site renewable investments are long-term investments. As such, financial expectations of a project will depend on expectations of how energy prices will vary over this longer time period. As with many observers, we see energy prices trending upwards in the long term as global demand continues to grow, energy supply becomes stretched, and much-needed but costly investments in ageing generating and grid infrastructure are carried out.

For companies with a large demand for electricity, such as the manufacturing, industrial or consumer goods sectors, security of energy supply is a critical issue and can be considered both in terms of physical supply and risk exposure to wholesale markets. To counter price volatility, on-site generation provides certainty that power can be produced at a certain price thus reducing exposure to price fluctuations. This exposure can be further reduced by integrating renewables with on-site storage or demand-side management services.

The second aspect of energy security becomes particularly pertinent when business operations are situated in a location with a poor grid infrastructure, or with inadequate transmission or generation capabilities. On-site renewable generation is able to compete directly with back-up generators to supply a cost-effective solution to insecure energy supply.

Extending this further, you quickly start to look to decentralized renewable energy investment as an enabler across rapidly growing economies, not only providing local economic benefits but also providing secure supply to regions that are remote from a centralized electricity infrastructure. This will play a vital role in sustainable development and poverty alleviation.

As you progress through these three aspects of the energy trilemma, there is an increasing engineering and technical challenge to ensure the effective integration of renewable solutions, storage and back-up generation, however the economic and social value created also increase markedly.

Despite a highly compelling argument for the consideration of renewable technologies on-site, it is important to understand that businesses face some key challenges. Crucial among these is the challenge of allocating capital to fund what can be a high upfront investment. Often a trade-off is presented that puts business expansion against investment in a renewable project. However, with the financing options that are available, this does not have to be the case.

The second challenge is one of allocating internal time. Planning processes, resource assessments, and site-level considerations are central to ensuring a viable project. However they can be time-consuming to manage and deliver. Getting the right expertise at the right time is critical to minimize project risks, and identifying expertise that has a track record in the sector is vital. Creating headline figures that have little or no grounding on practical experience is easy. Having a partner that has been through their own projects and re-applied their learning to that process is incredibly valuable as they will have learnt from experience the key considerations in calculating resource estimates and navigating the planning process or site considerations that need to be evaluated as an immediate priority.

The third challenge is then engaging with the supply chain. Whilst attractive to the site, on-site renewable solutions may be less attractive to suppliers. Given a choice of projects, suppliers naturally target scale and volume. Securing access to the supply chain and the ability to negotiate appropriate contractual terms will depend on the technology, but is also a challenge that can be easily underestimated.

Renewable energy options for powering business

Whether companies have a carbon-saving target or want to reduce their dependency on energy from fossil fuels – for cost, fuel scarcity, environmental or legislative reasons, making an investment in renewable energy generation can provide both short- and long-term benefits.

These benefits can be applied by either implementing renewable technologies on or near to existing buildings. This on-site approach provides excellent financial benefits, reducing the cost of distributing power onto the grid and shrinking the amount of fuel or power needed to be brought onto site (cutting utility bills significantly). In addition, making renewable energy generation a priority for new developments or for office expansion means avoiding any business disruption during installation. Once technology on a site has been investigated, then solutions off-site should be considered and are of increasing interest to businesses around the world. Below is a brief overview of some of the options: wind, solar and biomass (for heating and combined heat and power).

Wind

The use of wind power in the business community for commercial purposes is growing. As the technology undergoes continuous improvement, onshore wind has quickly become a cost-effective addition to a renewable energy portfolio. Furthermore, it provides a very visible sign to customers and competitors of a company's commitment to sustainability.

In addition to on-site turbines, companies are benefiting from wind by using off-site wind power options. This approach gives the same benefits of green energy and long-term electricity price security, but without the need of 'homing' an asset.

Solar

Solar photovoltaic (PV) is a simple, scalable technology with a vast array of different designs and applications. It is suitable for roof-mounting on new and existing buildings or can be deployed ground-mounted.

As a robust and proven technology, solar PV has many benefits. Its design is flexible and unobtrusive, with a simple and quick installation time and relatively low maintenance costs. In terms of financing, solar PV has 'bankable' and predictable financial returns, potentially making properties more rentable. In addition, solar PV may also improve the energy performance of buildings, leading to further savings.

Biomass heat

Biomass heat generation is a sustainable and secure energy choice. Using an abundant, reliable fuel and tried-and-tested technology, biomass heating can help meet renewable energy targets, cut greenhouse gas emissions and provide a reliable and secure heat supply for homes and businesses. Retrofitted biomass heating systems often work in conjunction with the existing fossil fuel heating system (such as natural gas or fuel oil boilers). The new biomass boiler then becomes the 'lead boiler', drastically cutting the use of fossil fuel on site, but still having the back-up of the old fossil fuel system. This approach can deliver surprisingly large financial benefits with minimal disruption. Optimum system sizing, good design and experienced consultants and contractors are the keys to success.

Biomass fuels come from a variety of sustainable sources including forestry residues, sawmill co-products, recycled wood and dedicated energy crops. They can be used to provide energy for a wide range of applications – from domestic heating to large-scale industrial heat and power generation. Wood and other biomass fuels are significant resources which re-absorb carbon as they grow through the process of photosynthesis.

Combined heat and power (CHP)

CHP can use a variety of renewable feedstock to produce both electricity and heat. For example, sites with very high heat demand such as industrial processes or district heating (communities and businesses connected by a heat main) can use wood chips to make large quantities of biomass heat and power, whilst smaller sites like a care home may benefit from a small natural gas CHP unit.

The choice of technology and the type of fuel depends on the amount of heat and temperature required. Similarly to biomass heat, success requires considerable expertise in respect to optimum system sizing and good design.

Effective energy management

Implementing on-site renewable energy solutions should always be considered as a part of a strategic approach to energy and cost reduction that includes energy saving and carbon management initiatives. This strategy should be based on an up-to-date review of business operations and site investment plans. This can ensure that the on-site investments are linked to wider strategic initiatives and a changing market.

Establishing a carbon baseline will provide a benchmark against which to measure and report progress, embedding change into the organization's practices and procedures to ensure ongoing compliance with changing legislation and continuous improvement. Taking a holistic approach to sustainability can give a business the maximum advantage in the transition to a low carbon and socially responsible economy.

Towards the future – a greener outlook for business?

The dual task of mitigating and adapting to climate change presents us with both opportunities and challenges. It is clear that more and more companies are exploiting the benefits of developing renewable energy portfolios, and we hope to see this trend continue in the coming years.

Business has the potential to lead the way in the transition to a low carbon economy. If your organization has the carbon and energy security drivers, and the desire to consider a portfolio of low carbon investments, some form of on-site generation could take a leading role in your switch to a greener future.

David Handley leads the advisory team at RES, one of the world's leading renewable energy developers. The team provides commercial, technical and strategic advice on renewable energy to businesses, communities and organizations around the world.

Further details: tel: 01923 299 200; e-mail: **advisory@res-ltd.com**.

Researcher: Stephanie Barraclough.

Notes

1 NOAA National Climatic Data Center (2013) State of the Climate: Global analysis for November 2013, [Online] http://www.ncdc.noaa.gov/sotc/global/2013/11.

2 Semrau, K (2013) Business can pave the way for renewable energy in the US, [Online] http://www.theguardian.com/sustainable-business/business-renewable-future.

3 GreenWise (2013) Onsite renewable generation to meet 14 per cent of UK's energy needs by 2030, [Online] http://www.greenwisebusiness.co.uk/news/onsite-renewable-generation-to-meet-14-per-cent-of-uks-energy-needs-by-2030-4153.aspx#.Ut-6UtLFLak.

PART TWO
The potential for innovation

Low-carbon growth

Collaboration through the supply chain can cut emissions and fuel growth.
Andy Eastlake, managing director of the Low Carbon Vehicle Partnership
(LowCVP), draws out the lessons from the automotive experience of
the clean-tech revolution.

The warnings from scientists have become increasingly clear – they indicate that the world has reached a tipping point in the way it uses natural resources to generate growth sustainably. Driven by concerns over resource scarcity, global warming and long-term affordability, sufficient momentum is building in consumer attitudes, business strategies and political willpower to make sustainable transport in the UK a viable proposition for those considering its adoption as well as offering potentially lucrative opportunities for investors.

The rising demand for mobility, increasing fuel prices and a favourable policy landscape is shaping Western European markets in favour of much lower carbon, ultra-efficient forms of transport. The UK in particular has emerged as a major driving force behind the growth of the low carbon vehicle market, and a major player in the research, development and deployment of electric and other vehicle technologies. For example, Nissan chose to produce the battery electric Leaf at its Sunderland plant, while Toyota produces the hybrid Auris and Ford its EcoBoost engines in the UK. There are plenty of other examples.

The policy backdrop

Responsible for around 20 per cent of carbon emissions, road transport is an important focus of policy initiatives designed to mitigate climate change.

Underpinning these in the UK is the 2008 Climate Change Act, which enshrines in law the commitment to virtually decarbonize all areas of the economy by 2050. A series of government Carbon Plans, reviewed by the Committee on Climate Change, are setting interim targets on the road to 2050.

European policy has been an important driver of developments. A 2015 target sets a mandatory obligation on manufacturers to cut average new car CO_2 emissions to below 130g/km CO_2 (a threshold the UK met in 2013). A follow-on target requires the achievement of an average 95g/km CO_2 by 2020/21. Subsequent targets are in the early stages of discussion but will inevitably continue to challenge the technology.

The UK has maintained a concerted and consistent policy approach – at least in terms of the development and adoption of a low carbon vehicle market – with a wide range of fiscal and other policy measures designed to incentivize low carbon vehicle uptake.

These have included the introduction of a carbon basis for taxation, including for company car tax, vehicle excise duty (VED) and fuel tax; the provision of innovation and investment support (via the Technology Strategy Board and other bodies) and latterly, national grant and subsidy programmes providing purchases subsidies for vehicles (plug-in car/van grants) and for recharging infrastructure ('Plugged-In Places'), together with a raft of local initiatives to encourage low carbon vehicles in use.

The Government is currently consulting on how to focus its spending following the significant commitment to invest another £500 million to encourage further adoption up to 2020, with initiatives likely to be aimed primarily at vehicle electrification; seen by the government as, perhaps, the main route to significant decarbonization of the car fleet.

The Green Bus Fund (GBF), running since 2010, has provided £100 million investment into the UK automotive industry and bus operators receive a further incentive from the Bus Service Operators' Grant (BSOG) rebate for low emission buses. The UK is now one of the leading adopters of low carbon buses with most of the vehicles being introduced, also made locally.

A 'virtuous circle'

A consistently-applied strategy – which has cross-party support and has survived change of governments – underpinned by a concerted, partnership-based approach to policy development is increasingly being seen to have delivered encouraging results suggesting that we can achieve both 'green' and growth.

The average CO_2 emissions of new cars sold in the UK has been reduced by nearly a quarter in the last decade (30 per cent since 2000). Car drivers have benefited with average vehicle fuel consumption per household down by about 18 per cent from 2002–12, improved fuel efficiency helping to moderate cost of living rises elsewhere.

High-profile UK investments such as those by Nissan, Toyota, Ford, Jaguar Land Rover and many others in low-emission technology and vehicles created the impression of vibrancy in the UK's low carbon automotive sector. Indeed, it is now widely perceived that the UK automotive sector and its supply chain industries have been bright spots in an otherwise austere UK economic picture in recent years.

Apart from car production, the UK has been among European and world leaders in the development and deployment of low emission buses. Prompted by the Green Bus Funds 1 to 4, there are now around 1500 in operation in the country.

There has been activity too in the development of low-carbon technologies for use in commercial vehicle operations and a growing focus on decarbonizing these larger vehicles through a range of measures.

The UK's approach to policy-making in the last decade or so has been characterized by structured efforts to engage industry, consumer and environment groups and other stakeholders in the development of policy and information. Industry works closely with the government's business department (Department for Business, Innovation and Skills – BIS) through the Automotive Council, while the Department for Transport (DfT) is the main funder of the uniquely broad stakeholder, Low Carbon Vehicle Partnership (LowCVP). With the Department of Energy and Climate Change (DECC) and the Department for Environment, Food and Rural Affairs (DEFRA) also active in transport energy and environmental impacts, plus of course the Treasury managing the fiscal measures, this sector touches almost every area of society and government.

Technology options and cost efficiency

Currently (Spring 2014), there are 18 electric and plug-in cars and 9 vans eligible for a £5,000 (£8,000 for vans) discount through the government's plug-in vehicle programme. Model options are increasing fast, offering features that will suit a growing range of operational requirements. Though purchase costs are still generally higher than conventional vehicles, fleet and transport managers need to make decisions based not just on purchase but on the total cost of ownership which can lead to different conclusions in terms of technology choices.

Almost all 'conventional' gasoline and diesel engines also now incorporate a range of low carbon and energy saving features from 'stop-start' to lightweight components, energy harvesting and dashboard indicators to encourage 'eco-driving'. As tax and running costs are a considerable proportion of all costs, the total cost of ownership should also be the paramount factor when making purchase choices. It would be reasonable to assume that the 'cost of carbon' as signalled in tax instruments is also likely to rise over time.

With fuel costs also on a generally upward trajectory, making the lowest carbon vehicle choice is an obvious one as low carbon goes hand-in-hand with lower fuel consumption.

Apart from electrification, there are a range of other alternative fuel choices possible and indeed practical, particularly for fleets operating out of a depot or fixed base and those requiring longer distance journeys. Gaseous fuels – natural gas, both liquid (LNG) and compressed (CNG) including biomethane, LPG – as well as some biofuels (and, since the latest Budget, methanol) enjoy fiscal support and provide a wide range of options for reducing carbon and running costs from both existing and new vehicles across the whole road transport sector and beyond.

Conclusion

The 'clean-tech' revolution is well under way in the road transport sector. Supportive international and national government policy and funding has acted to rapidly reduce tailpipe carbon emissions and improve vehicle running costs despite a multitude of competing pressures in air quality, safety and customer comfort expectations. Moreover the UK (and partners in the EU) are seeing opportunities for export and growth and are investing in the low carbon automotive technologies, through the innovation supply chain, which are expected to dominate the international markets of the future.

There is a comprehensive range of low carbon vehicles available to fleet buyers and consumers from improved 'conventional' types to inspirational new technologies. Most forward-looking fleet operators are keeping a close eye on this rapidly evolving situation and increasingly opting to purchase vehicles that cut carbon and, importantly, operating costs.

The UK's collaborative approach to the challenge has created a unique respect across all the organizations with a stake in the road transport sector. Many are choosing to become more closely involved in the drive to accelerate the shift to low carbon vehicles and fuels.

The LowCVP was set up by the Government in 2003 to engage all stakeholders in discussions, to find better policy solutions and develop other initiatives for cutting overall carbon emissions from road transport; a particularly hard nut to crack given the long-term trend of growth in vehicle usage.

The Partnership – which now has approaching 200 member organizations – is tasked not only with delivering road transport emissions reductions but also with safeguarding the economic benefits provided to UK plc by the automotive sector and, in particular, to help place local businesses at the forefront of the low carbon shift.

The LowCVP provides members with the opportunity to connect with key stakeholders, including local authorities, central government, motor and energy companies, environment groups, user communities and others; to collaborate with them in the development of policy and other initiatives and, ultimately, to influence the future development of the road transport sector.

For more information please visit: **www.lowcvp.org.uk/about/how-to-join.htm** or contact: **secretariat@lowcvp.org.uk.**

Smarter buildings

Richard Solomon at KSR Architects considers the latest technologies for smarter control of buildings.

The wide range of alternative energy solutions available, combined with the influence of legislation and regulation, has sent the construction industry scurrying in various directions. Our clients – both residential and commercial – have a desire to demonstrate their green credentials but oftentimes have little understanding of the complexity involved in integrating clean tech into their schemes.

Whether it is because we genuinely want to save the planet, or if it is just to keep our souls clean, we all want a simple, straightforward way of using green technology in our buildings. And we have every right to expect one. Nowadays we are all living more technology-rich lives. We enjoy browsing and roaming free from technical constraint and are used to having both choice and fingertip control over how, where and when we consume multi-media content. What's more, we are increasingly looking for this functionality in our homes. We are starting to find 'the internet of things' impacting our lives.

It's clear from the level of activity in this space that there is a large and growing market for simple smart home equipment – many homeowners who struggled with multiple connected devices in the past are enjoying driving their Sonos music system from their smart phone or controlling their boiler using British Gas's Hive application in a similar way. Google's acquisition of Nest probably says more about their need for strong product design than anything else, but it is indicative of confidence in the 'smarthome'. So what can designers and builders learn from all this?

We're undoubtedly moving towards an age of smarter homes in smarter cities. The face of the high street is changing in response to the developing internet-based retail experience. We'll see public services like mass transit and waste collection optimized through the use of inexpensive, connected sensors and the rise in 'quantified self' adoption (people using fitness or healthcare devices like the Nike+ Fuelband or Sony's new Lifelog products) will soon allow people with long-term chronic conditions like diabetes to benefit from accurate monitoring and care with little friction in their daily lives. This in turn means we'll be able to provide building users with simple interfaces to control and monitor their energy use in a way they understand.

In many of the higher-end homes we've designed, clients are using simple touch-panel controls from companies like AMX. But these can be expensive, and rely on sophisticated programming and careful integration with the lighting, heating, cooling and other systems. We're now seeing a trend where people prefer to operate things from their smart phone or iPad. In turn many manufacturers are producing affordable equipment with the integration interface built right in. Heatmiser and Philips are two good examples of this. And increasingly, the systems can sense occupancy – which means they can be driven by actual demand, not the old-school timer under the stairs.

So it feels like the future is in reach, but there are still a few challenges.

Integration is key

Most energy consumption in developed nations is used in homes for heating, lighting and home electronics, but a unified approach will allow these functions to be centrally controlled and intelligently managed. Integrated control stops heating and cooling systems 'fighting', making everything work much more efficiently. The right approach is to ensure the building can relate to local temperature, weather information from the internet, or react to a regular in-room thermostat. Modern lighting control systems allow artificial lighting to react to the levels of daylight (as well as occupancy). Local scene-setting switches can be provided to help our clients save energy and get the quality of light they need without wastage. It's also possible to use automated blinds to reduce glare and minimize solar gain, avoiding the need for cooling. Taken together, these steps can make a massive difference to the overall energy consumption as well as enhance the quality and enjoyment of a home.

There are various standards in place to allow the systems to 'talk' to each other and most kit can be controlled wirelessly these days or over a simple network connection. The key is to plan early to avoid disappointment and costly refits, and to find an inspirational services consultant, such as SMC, that acts as a client advocate – solving this in the 'nerdosphere' isn't going to help the people that use the building.

At a recently completed luxury private house in London, we worked with SMC and the client from an early stage to ensure that the technology could be integrated seamlessly and effortlessly into the building design. The highly sophisticated systems were specified and located as part of the design development. Chosen elements which brought together audio-visual, security and environmental control were selected to be intuitive as well as aesthetically pleasing.

The business case

There is undoubtedly an initial premium attached to smart buildings, however, the return on investment (ROI) can be significant. Specifying the right building control system is often key to how quickly this ROI is realized. A centralized control system will not only ensure that a family or an organization gets the most out of its technological investment, but that this investment continues to pay dividends over the lifetime of the building. This means that our clients can look for ways to spread the cost of intelligent, green systems, and bundle it in with maintenance and support. With the right approach it doesn't all need to be capital expenditure (CAPEX). We've found that disparate estates can be simply managed from a central location nowadays.

Whilst we haven't found a particular building size below which it is uneconomical to install smart technology, we do know that reducing complexity is beneficial. That means getting our clients to engage with the design process, and to consider how they'll actually use the building. This allows them to make considered and beneficial decisions, naturally with some guidance on the way and here's where experts such as SMC play such a key role.

Create a great customer experience

A good green installation is no more obtrusive than traditional systems, but sometimes the interface needs more consideration, and one thing has never changed – all our customers hate complex controls, particularly when they're duplicated across many systems. People pay for simplicity and in my experience, simpler systems are more reliable – and cheaper to run. We've found it useful to work with a customer-focused integration company. They'll think about what control our clients would be most comfortable with – a simple light switch in the bathroom, perhaps a scene-setting keypad in the bedroom, or a touchscreen in the family room – and come up with a control solution that fits. Our clients can have access to all system functions, or just what they want. The integrator will programme the system to suit and customize the interface accordingly, even if it's run on their iPad, so that our clients are left with an intuitive and easy-to-operate solution.

Richard Solomon's enthusiasm for architecture was fuelled by studying at the Architectural Association under internationally renowned architects, Rem Koolhaas and Zaha Hadid. He is the partner with overall management responsibilities within the practice, playing a significant role in maintaining its high quality of design and expanding the client base. Having worked closely with developers for over 30 years, Richard has a commercial understanding of all aspects of development, particularly in the residential sector. He believes passionately in new, innovative approaches to design, system building and sustainability. Currently working on projects in Russia and China, Richard is widely travelled. He enjoys adventure and loves nothing more than cycling amongst the wildlife of Botswana.

Further information is available from: Richard Solomon
A A Dip RIBA, Partner, KSR Architects (tel: 020 7692 5000; e-mail: **richard.solomon@ksrarchitects.com**; website: **www.ksrarchitects.com**) and Steve Moore, SMC (tel: 020 7819 1700; e-mail: **steve@smc-uk.com**; website: **www.smc-uk.com**).

Efficiency gains

Andrew Mitchell at the CleanWeb Factory considers energy efficiency as a driver for innovation and investment.

The cleanest, cheapest and most renewable form of energy is not using it in the first place, ie energy efficiency. With global political tensions rising over the supply of oil and gas, it's by far the most secure form of energy too.

In their August 2013 report, 'Shining a light: uncovering the business energy efficiency opportunity' the Confederation of British Industry (CBI) suggest that domestic and non-domestic energy efficiency could boost the UK GDP by at least 1 per cent. Additionally they estimate a potential UK energy efficiency market opportunity of £17.6 billion.

In some cases the cost of implementing energy efficiency can be zero. For example turning your home thermostat down by 1 degree can save you around £75 and 310 kilograms carbon dioxide (CO_2) a year (according to the Energy Savings Trust). In other cases, significant investment in research, development and commercialization is required, which then has enormous potential across an entire industry or industries. Take for instance the 2014 introduction in Formula One of new engines, an evolved 'Energy Recovery System' (which generates energy from braking and waste heat from the engine), and limiting fuel to 100 kilograms per race. This is a tough challenge to the best technical brains in motorsport and academia to innovate and find energy efficiencies. Previous Formula One innovations, such as turbo engines, safer tyres, carbon-fibre chassis and traction control systems have a strong track-record of transferring to everyday road vehicles.

Investment

There are some significant challenges with energy efficiency, one being human nature and changing consumer behaviour. Another relates to venture capital and other forms of investment. Investors can't always physically grasp energy efficiency like they can other forms of clean tech; and it's not always clear and 'controllable' who reaps the financial benefit – obviously a key priority with any investor.

I had the privilege of being invited to the White House in Washington DC in 2012 and 2013 to participate as an investor guest in the US Department of Energy's National Business Plan Competition. In 2012, President Obama's Chief Technology Officer led a panel discussion on the state of clean tech investment. Robin Chase, the founder of car-sharing company, Buzzcar (resource efficiency), stressed that energy efficiency is such a 'big prize' but it is being ignored by investors. She was right, but I believe things are improving. In 2013's equivalent panel we were gifted hot tips from two legends of the clean energy revolution, Professor Dan Reicher and Mike Ahearn. Stanford University's Dan Reicher is the former Energy and Climate Director of Google Inc. and has served in the US Government under three Presidents. Mike Ahearn from True North Venture Partners is the founder of NASDAQ-listed First Solar, the first pure play renewable energy company to be listed on Standard & Poor's 500 stock market index. Mike Ahearn's hot tip was to get in to 'massively distributed' energy generation; bringing power and heat to communities off the grid and reducing pressure on the grid. Dan Reicher's hot tip for where young ambitious entrepreneurs and brave investors should get in to is energy efficiency. Add to this the view from Khosla Ventures's Andrew Chung, that corporate venturing is going to save clean tech, I think there is a very bright future in energy efficiency ventures. Khosla Ventures has a US $3 billion fund with 80-plus sustainability companies in their portfolio.

Going back to the tip of turning your home thermostat down by 1 degree, the second runner-up of the British Gas 'Connecting Homes Startup Competition' in London, September 2013, was a venture called OpenTRV. OpenTRV have a very neat proposition that enables you to set and control temperature in individual rooms, through a simple internet-enabled thermostat, retrofitted to existing radiators. Personally I think they should have won the competition, and this is a great example of an energy efficiency venture that corporate venturing outfits and VCs can make sense of.

The UK's Green Investment Bank (GIB) is another encouraging example of energy efficiency as an investment strategy and business opportunity. Energy efficiency is one of the GIB's four priority areas, the other three being offshore wind, waste recycling and energy from waste. In 2012/2013 this 'for-profit bank' invested £150 million in energy efficiency ventures, out of a total investment portfolio of £635 million; approximately 24 per cent of their portfolio. The GIB is leveraging their initial £3.8 billion fund too. For example, in February 2014 the GIB announced a £50 million alliance (£25 million each) with the Société Générale Equipment Finance, to invest in energy efficiency projects. Mainstream corporate finance is active in energy efficiency too. In 2012 the Royal Bank of Scotland (RBS) launched a £200 million 'Carbon Reduction Fund' and The London Energy Efficiency Fund has been established with £100 million to invest in energy efficiency retrofits to public, private and voluntary sector buildings and infrastructure. At the 'angel' end of the spectrum, leading syndicates such as Archangel Informal Investment have an active portfolio of relevant companies (eg Ewgeco, Oxy-Gen Combustion, Flexitricity). The point here is, there are plentiful business opportunities in energy efficiency with an abundance of venture finance across the spectrum from angel investment to structured corporate finance.

Waste

The highest barrier to energy efficiency, in economies such as the UK, I would argue is apathy and relative wealth. We waste an enormous amount of food, water, heat and electricity in the UK, each of which have significant carbon footprints. The 'Waste and Resources Action Programme' suggest that 15 million tonnes of food went to waste in the UK in 2010 and according to Tesco's own published figures, 28,500 tonnes of food were wasted in their stores and distribution centres in the first six months of 2013. Tesco also estimate that many UK families waste at least £700 of food per year. All of this is scandalous, considering the energy cost of food production, processing, distribution and disposal.

In a relatively wealthy country such as the UK, I would argue that money is not a motivator to change consumer behaviour. If it were, wouldn't we have witnessed a reduction in energy consumption as the 'credit crunch' gripped us over 2007 to 2012? As you can see in Table 2.3.1 from data published by the Department of Energy and Climate Change, other than a dip in 2008, the UK continues to use more and more energy every year. In my mind, to change consumer behaviour, we either need more and more cataclysmic weather events and resulting economic impact that the majority of people accept are caused by man-made climate change; OR we need a technology-push solution. Which is why the field of 'energy informatics' is so important.

TABLE 2.3.1   Energy consumption in the UK 2007–2012

Year	UK domestic electricity consumption*
2007	5.5 mtoe
2008	4.9 mtoe
2009	6.2 mtoe
2010	5.5 mtoe
2011	6.3 mtoe
2012	6.7 mtoe

* Million tonnes of oil equivalent (mtoe) adjusted and temperature corrected.
SOURCE: Department of Energy and Climate Change 'Energy Consumption in the UK (2013)'.
Publication URN: 13D/154 Published: 25 July 2013.

Andrew Mitchell is Managing Director of CleanWeb Factory Ltd, a company that delivers executive education and innovation programmes for high-growth ventures, corporates and public sector leaders. Andrew is a programme manager with 19 years' experience in the ICT sector and 12 years' experience in business-university collaboration and commercialization. He has worked for small businesses, FTSE100 corporations and world leading research-intensive universities; internationally in Scotland, England, Spain, North America, Australia, China and India. From 2011 to 2013, he was a business manager at the Edinburgh Centre for Carbon Innovation, a 30 million-euro 'low carbon innovation hub'. Prior to this he established and grew Informatics Ventures, based in Europe's largest and Britain's highest-quality computer science department.

Further details: mobile: 07793 111386;

e-mail: **andrew.mitchell@cleanwebfactory.com**;

Twitter: **http://twitter.com/roomitchell**; website: **www.cleanwebfactory.com**.

Changes in corporate behaviour

Directors are assuming control for environmental impact and are reviewing how best to adopt clean technology. **Matt Bonass** at Bird & Bird explains why.

Companies have been embracing the green economy for some time now. The world's largest companies, such as General Electric (GE), Google and Microsoft, have each placed sustainability at the heart of their strategy. GE have created 'GE Citizenship' to promote sustainability.[1] Google have adopted their 'Google Green' programme.[2] Microsoft state their 'citizenship' role as follows:

1 Minimize the environmental impact of our business operations and products.

2 Create technology solutions that help individuals and businesses around the world address their environmental impact.'[3]

This prompts the question: why do companies such as these act in this way? What motivates their behaviour?

Corporate behaviour is constantly evolving. There is no doubt that much action is voluntary and taken with the best environmental intentions. When asked, directors of companies will tell you that they are keen to minimize the effects of climate change, to preserve resources and to adopt renewable sources of energy – where proportionate of course. However, a more cynical observer would argue that significantly more action is taken because companies are being forced to act. Or because companies recognize the economic consequences of inaction.

Directors and shareholders are alive to the demands of the public, the ultimate consumers of goods and services offered by their companies. This generally influences corporate behaviour in a positive way. One example of this is the drive by boards to increase the proportion of female directors on company boards, as has been recommended by the UK Government.

So, how is positive sustainable behaviour influenced at board level? Much has been written about the art of motivation and driving motivation through 'carrots' (ie, rewards) or 'sticks' (ie, punishments). This article therefore considers some of the 'carrots' and 'sticks' that are influencing boardroom behaviour, drawing on some examples which are prevalent in the UK.

Directors' duties under company law

It is a fundamental principle of UK company law that a director of a UK company must act in the way he considers, in good faith, would be most likely to promote the success of the company for the benefit of its members as a whole.[4] In doing so, they are required, where relevant and in so far as is reasonably practicable, to take into account certain non-exhaustive factors. As of 1 October 2007, one such factor which was added to the Companies Act was the requirement for a director to consider 'the impact of the company's operations on the community and the environment'.[5] Explanatory notes to the legislation made it clear that 'it will not be sufficient to pay lip service to [the factors] and in many cases the directors will need to take action to comply with this aspect of the duty'.[6]

So, a company wishes to engage a new service provider. Service provider A is a little more expensive but has excellent sustainability criteria. Service provider B is cheaper but pays no heed to sustainability. What is a director supposed to do?

There is limited UK case law on the point, not least as any actions for breach may only be 'derivative', ie can only be brought by shareholders, and not by the general public as a stakeholder for the environment. It is clear from commentary that making decisions based purely on the financial business case without heed to the environment or the community would not be satisfactory. However, it is equally clear that a director will not be expected to compromise the commercial interests of the company to achieve environmental aims.[7]

What is beyond doubt though is that the introduction of a requirement under UK company law to consider the environment and community has required boards to take much more care in assessing environmental issues, which has naturally led to a change of corporate behavioural practices.

Mandatory disclosure of environmental emissions

There has for some years been limited voluntary disclosure by companies of their greenhouse gas emissions. One example of this is the UK Carbon Disclosure Project (CDP) which seeks to publish carbon emissions information which it receives from participants and which it considers relevant to potential investors.[8] Participants can sense the 'carrot': using disclosure of their environmental credentials as a marketing tool.

We have recently seen legislation in the UK that moves away from voluntary disclosure towards mandatory disclosure – replacing the 'carrot' with the 'stick'. Two examples of this are set out below.

Disclosure in directors' reports

From October 2013 and for financial years ending on or after 30 September 2013, quoted companies[9] are required to report annual greenhouse gas emissions from activities for which they are responsible on a worldwide basis as part of their directors' report. These emissions must be benchmarked against the previous year's emissions. Disclosure is made on a 'comply or explain' basis – there is scope for companies to explain non-reporting to the extent it was not practical to obtain the information. Sanctions for failure to report include court proceedings to enforce compliance.

So far so good, but there have been criticisms of the regulations – the 'stick' is not sufficiently sharp. They only relate to quoted companies, whereas they should relate to a certain size threshold of company. There are not presently any requirements to report on emissions associated with inputs (such as emissions from the supply chain) or outputs (such as emissions from products when used by customers). There should be independent verification of the information reported and an explicit requirement to consider what scope there is to reduce emissions. Finally, sectors should apply the same methodology of reporting to ease effective comparisons. The legislation is in its early days. Notwithstanding the wrinkles, mandatory reporting is in the author's view clearly a step in the right direction.

The UK Carbon Reduction Commitment Energy Efficiency Scheme (CRC)

The CRC is the UK's mandatory emissions trading scheme for large businesses and public sector organizations. Introduced in April 2010, it has undergone a number of changes not least in the commencement of its initial phase, now 1 April 2014.

Organizations are required to participate where they meet certain qualification criteria, broadly as to the amount of megawatts of qualifying electricity supplied through settled half-hourly metering. The scheme requires participating organizations to buy carbon allowances, to put in place systems to collate data about their energy use and CO_2 emissions and report this on an annual basis. Its aim is to provide public and private sector participants with an incentive to reduce their emissions.

The CRC therefore represents another 'stick' to motivate behaviour. However, it did also include two 'carrots'. When introduced, the Environment Agency (as scheme administrator) was required to publish a 'league table' ranking participants on their emissions reductions. It was proposed that any revenue generated from the sale of carbon allowances would be 'recycled' back to participants based on their ranking in the league tables. In 2010, the UK government announced that the revenue raised from the sale of allowances would not be recycled to the best performing participants but would be used instead to support public finances – ie, it effectively became a tax. In 2012, the government announced that the league tables would be abolished. The author considers it a great shame that participants no longer compete to top the league table – retailers such as Tesco and Sainsbury took their rankings very seriously. In times of austerity, the government has chosen on this occasion to take away the 'carrots'.

'Greening' the supply chain

Companies are increasingly looking to manage their supply chain in a sustainable manner, including Walmart, L'Oréal, Jaguar and National Grid. For example, a company may place emissions reduction targets on suppliers and freeze them out if they do not comply.

The UK Carbon Disclosure Project (CDP), together with Accenture, has for the last six years published a supply chain report.[10] The 2013/14 report generated responses from nearly 3,000 companies. The report makes clear that suppliers and customers are collaborating to drive down carbon emissions: 56 per cent of customers reported that their ultimate consumers were becoming more receptive to low-carbon products and services. The report also notes that suppliers and customers have a real opportunity to build both revenue and brand along the way. Initiatives such as the CDP report are affecting the way in which boards approach contracting with suppliers.

Renewable energy generation

In addition, the largest companies in the world are investing in on-site renewable generation, particularly through solar and wind. Detailed commentary on the subsidies that attach to renewable energy generation are outside the scope of this article, but they are not insignificant when factored against the concerns of security of supply and price volatility.

Google is a leading example. It aims to power 100 per cent of its company with renewable energy – they are currently at 34 per cent.[11] They have invested over US $1 billion in renewable energy projects to date.

Greenpeace commented as follows on Google:

> Google has been the most open in the industry about the importance of increasing not only energy efficiency within the sector, but also the need to move our energy sources to renewable energy. Google has made significant efforts to increase the company's transparency. This is a great step forward... Google's commitment to using renewable energy as much as possible has set the bar for the industry.[12]

Opportunities for demand-side management and 'co-venturing'

We have seen above that organizations such as Google have realized that the green economy motivates behaviour to increase revenue and expand markets. Being more energy efficient can also reduce costs – something close to the heart of every finance director. As outlined in Table 3.3.1 in Michael Rudd's chapter (page 79) there are a variety of demand-side management solutions (including energy efficiency) that enable an organization to achieve cost reductions and a wide variety of other important objectives.

As well as focusing on renewable energy generation and energy efficiency, some companies are buying out niche technology players and merging them into their research and development teams. They are looking to develop new forms of energy management or renewable generation, such as tidal, wave, clean vehicles and energy storage. GE's 'Ecomagination' is a good example of this.[13]

Conclusion

Company boards face a choice in the green economy between action and inaction. Boards either look to embrace the changes and lead; or pass up the opportunity to adopt and fall behind their competitors.

Company actions must be genuine however, or be subject to ridicule: bold statements on sustainability may seem impressive but the public are becoming increasingly adept at spotting 'greenwashing'.[14] To be effective, any green reporting needs to be consistent, comparable, accurate, complete, relevant and reliable, as well as transparent.

Smart directors recognize that they can capitalize on opportunities to expand their market. They can smell the 'carrots', both in terms of energy subsidies and the opportunity to build revenue and brand. In addition, they appreciate that the 'sticks', such as environmental and carbon legislation, are only going to get longer and sharper and that positive action now could gain 'first mover' advantage and save costs in the long term.

It is clear that decisions on environmental issues are no longer the sole remit of the environmental manager. Boards of companies are now taking control of and managing their environmental impacts. Directors hope that this will enable them to achieve a reputational advantage, reduce operational costs (such as energy bills), face less exposure to volatile energy prices and identify new business opportunities.

Matt Bonass is a partner in Bird & Bird's corporate department. He specializes in public and private mergers and acquisitions (M&A), private equity, joint ventures and equity capital markets work, regularly advising boards of directors on corporate issues. He has particular expertise in the clean-tech and renewable energy and traditional fossil fuels-based energy sectors. He has advised governments, trading exchanges, financial institutions, venture capital and private equity houses, early stage clean-tech companies and major corporations on transactions in the oil and gas and electricity sectors and in the wind, solar, wave, biomass, biofuels, waste to energy, energy efficiency and carbon sectors.

Matt has been recognized as a leading individual in Chambers Legal Directory for a number of years in the fields of both climate change law and corporate finance as well as in Legal 500 for renewables and oil and gas. Together with Michael Rudd, he co-edited a book entitled *Renewables: A practical handbook* (Globe Law and Business, 2010). He is a member of the Institute of Directors.

The author would like to recognise the assistance given by Joanna Ketteley, a colleague in Bird & Bird's environmental team, in the preparation of this article.

Further details: tel: + 44 (0)20 7415 6731; e-mail: **matt.bonass@twobirds.com** website: **www.twobirds.com**

Notes

1 www.gecitizenship.com.

2 http://www.google.co.uk/green/.

3 http://www.microsoft.com/about/corporatecitizenship/en-us/working-responsibly/principled-business-practices/environmental-sustainability/.

4 Section 172, Companies Act 2006.

5 Section 172 (1) (d), Companies Act 2006.

6 http://www.legislation.gov.uk/ukpga/2006/46/notes/division/6/2.

7 *R v HM Treasury* [2009] EWHC 3020 (Admin).

8 https://www.cdp.net/en-US/Pages/HomePage.aspx.

9 ie, companies listed on the Main Market of the London Stock Exchange.

10 https://www.cdp.net/CDPResults/CDP-Supply-Chain-Report-2014.pdf.

11 http://www.google.co.uk/green/energy/.

12 http://www.google.co.uk/green/energy/.

13 http://www.ge.com/about-us/ecomagination.

14 ie, disingenuously spinning products and policies as environmentally friendly.

Clean options on major projects

Take an innovative approach to clean tech to cut the risk on major capital projects, say **Tom Woollard** and **Nick Cottam** at ERM.

Emerging economies continue to play a key role in the global economy. These economies are awash with natural resources but can also be infused with political and non-technical risk. For project developers, innovative project planning, including the consideration of clean tech solutions should be integral to their approach.

This is not always the case. Failure to recognize and react to non-technical risk is leading to significant and costly project delays (see below). Aside from the way projects get financed and engineered, there is every incentive to incorporate relevant clean-tech thinking.

Inevitably geographical priorities keep changing. In recent years, there has been tremendous interest in the accelerating influence of the BRIC (Brazil, Russia, India and China) countries, which in 2010 accounted for a quarter of the world's gross national income. Enter more recently still the MINT countries: Mexico, Indonesia, Nigeria and Turkey. Whether it's a BRIC or a MINT, capital-intensive natural resource projects play a key role in fuelling accelerated GDP growth.

Project delays

In 2012 ERM conducted an analysis of the causes of delays in major capital projects in the extractives sector. We reviewed nearly 200 projects, each with

FIGURE 2.5.1 Delayed extractive projects with CAPEX greater than $500m

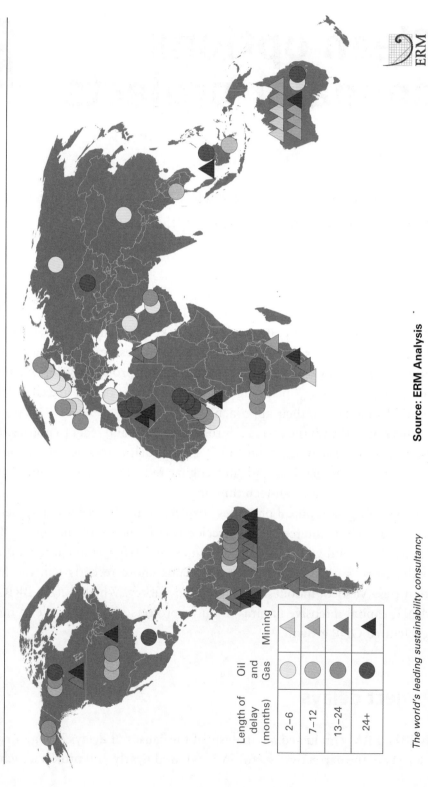

Length of delay (months)	Oil and Gas	Mining
2–6	⬤	◀
7–12	⬤	◀
13–24	⬤	◀
24+	⬤	◀

Source: ERM Analysis

The world's leading sustainability consultancy

a CAPEX of greater than US $500 million. We found that substantial delays ranging from 2 to 24 months had been reported in more than half of them (see Figure 2.5.1).

Whilst projects typically referred to more than one delay factor, it was clear that in oil and gas projects technical issues often play a critical role (22 per cent of delayed projects). See Figure 2.5.2.

Innovative project thinking

Several corporations have calculated the financial cost of these project delays, which can run into billions of US dollars. As a result they are seeking to integrate more innovative thinking around project risk – for example transport, natural resources, community engagement – at the earliest possible 'options analysis' phase of a project.

One example is the consideration of transport options when a project involves building a mine in a remote and environmentally sensitive location. In short, is there an alternative to road or rail options? The enlightened project team will look at using rivers/waterways, automated conveyor systems and even cable cars. In each case, they will weigh up both short- and long-term benefits, taking into account such factors as economic, social, environmental and reputational benefit. With proper 'clean tech' analysis, they might well reach the conclusion that there is a better alternative than 20 road trucks a day doing return journeys for the next 50 years.

Figure 2.5.3 illustrates the potential implications of not fully considering technical and non-technical risks at an early stage of the project lifecycle.

It's all in the planning

Major extractives projects take many years in the conceiving and multiple financial, technical (and in some cases) non-technical options are identified analysed, compared and prioritized at each stage of project planning. There are inevitably many competing demands on the project team from a wide range of stakeholders: corporate pressure to get the project up and running; governmental pressure to ensure that the project is compliant and will make a positive contribution to the region; local community pressure to give the project its 'social licence to operate'.

FIGURE 2.5.2 At least 53% of projects have experienced a delay

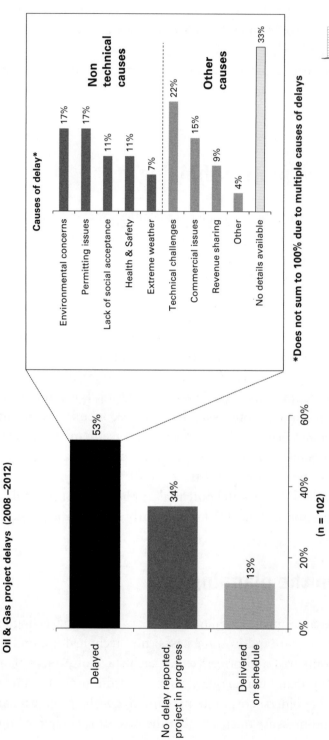

Oil & Gas project delays (2008 –2012)

Causes of delay*

Environmental concerns — 17%
Permitting issues — 17%
Lack of social acceptance — 11%
Health & Safety — 11%
Extreme weather — 7%

Non technical causes

Technical challenges — 22%
Commercial issues — 15%
Revenue sharing — 9%
Other — 4%
No details available — 33%

Other causes

*Does not sum to 100% due to multiple causes of delays

Delayed — 53%
No delay reported, project in progress — 34%
Delivered on schedule — 13%

0%   20%   40%   60%

(n = 102)

Source: ERM Analysis

The world's leading sustainability consultancy

FIGURE 2.5.3 Successful projects carefully consider all the alternatives

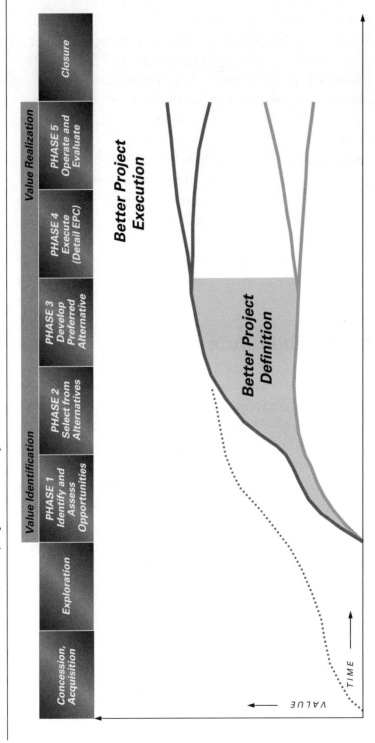

These pressures often combine to make the project team opt for the most conservative 'path of least resistance'. So the preferred option often looks remarkably like the project that went before it (the one where the costs were controlled and the engineering solutions are well known). This consistency – the 'business as usual' approach – can be immensely reassuring to planners and developers, leading to faster and less problematic planning, approval and commissioning. It can also inhibit and delay the adoption of clean technologies.

It is not always a question of 'new' clean technologies that need to be encouraged. Old clean technologies may play a useful role. The fuel-free funicular railway option for transporting material and people up and down steep inclines should be reassessed for certain types of project. In several countries 100-year-old, gravity-powered funicular railways are still in operation. Some major capital projects are also beginning to re-evaluate old (low impact) transport technologies such as barges and even airships.

Design for the future

Major capital projects have long-term usually permanent impacts. The roads, railways, mines, ports, refineries and chemical plants that are built today are likely to have a lifespan of up to 100 years. The challenge for developers and their stakeholders is to develop structures that will be acceptable for the rest of this century.

Over the last 40 years we have seen a huge change in society's willingness to accept industrial pollution from any source. When we look at industrial facilities built in the 1960s and 1970s we are shocked at the lack of attention paid to the impacts on the immediate environment and the local community. There has been a significant mind-set shift in terms of what is acceptable and desirable and this is not just in developed economies (eg the high-profile and damaging urban air and water quality concerns in Chinese and Indian mega-cities).

A clean tech blueprint

So what should developers be mindful of in the early stages of project development? Here is a blueprint for the longer term mind-set – an *innovation overlay* which this author believes should be applied to major capital and resource intensive projects:

- *Energy sources* – The options considered do not necessarily have to be innovative. Detailed and costed consideration should be given to tried-and-tested renewable technologies such as wind, solar, hydro and geothermal. Natural lighting, heating and cooling options should be comprehensively reviewed and assessed. Low energy equipment and materials, building design and positioning, natural insulation, etc can all be deployed to manage increasing energy costs.

- *Water* – Depending on the physical location, technologies that either reduce the consumption of fresh water, reduce the risk of flooding (eg involving a much wider water catchment management) and that prevent the discharge of contaminated effluent (eg zero-discharge facilities). Much greater attention should be paid to catchment planning, rainwater harvesting, low energy treatment, efficient desalination, advanced smart metering, leakage detection, water-saving devices, hydro-kinetic and potential energy recovery and low energy water treatment. There is a huge array of technologies to reduce demand, increase supplies or simply reduce costs.

- *Waste* – Zero emission, discharge and waste facilities should be considered in highly sensitive environments; where this is not possible recycling and energy from waste (eg combustion, gasification, pyrolysis, etc) should be mandated. Options that eliminate or minimize waste at design, construction and most importantly operational phases of the life cycle should be prioritized. The long-term build-up of waste over the 50-plus-year project lifecycle will significantly impact decommissioning and closure costs as many companies have found to their cost.

- *Biodiversity* – For industry there is a fairly well-understood hierarchy for managing biodiversity impacts; avoidance (as part of the project planning) which is the best option, if this is not possible then the only options are to minimize, mitigate and offset the impact. Clean (low impact) technology plays a critical role in all of these options. The fact that some companies are exploring the concept of 'net positive impact' illustrates the ever-increasing importance of biodiversity. A range of clean technologies will be required to measure, monitor and reduce biodiversity impacts, while also compensating for loss.

- *Transport* – At the planning stage, considerable attention should be paid to the transport system (road, rail, air, water, etc.) and the long-term impacts of the choice of vehicles deployed (eg, electric cars, hydrogen fuel-celled vehicles, trams, etc).

- *Information technology and the workforce* – IT-enabled technologies have transformed business in the last 15 years. Not least the way that major capital projects are conceptualized, designed, planned, assessed, approved and implemented has changed fundamentally. Understanding what clean technologies are available and where they have been successfully deployed is now readily accessible to all decision-makers and stakeholders.

- *Non-technical risks* – water scarcity, community unrest, rare species, indigenous people's rights and heritage issues can all prevent or significantly delay major capital projects – the frequency and extent of these business impacts has only relatively recently been financially quantified and highlighted. Clean technologies may be the solution for some projects. For example, if the project is being carried out in an area of scarce water availability, rather than compete with the local communities for the limited resource, it may be better to identify a way in which the facility could generate water (eg, rainwater harvesting or investing in desalination).

'Flagship' projects

These often come about because of the anticipated public scrutiny. Extractive projects in areas of high biodiversity or in areas where indigenous peoples reside are frequently forced (by political and locational circumstances) to use cleaner technology. Because of the sensitivity of the surrounding environment, these projects may develop low consumption, low impact technologies (often more fully automated and with reduced workforces) and innovative infrastructure solutions that avoid harm to the environment and local inhabitants. It is unfortunate that in less sensitive habitats where clean, low impact innovations are not demanded by regulators and civil society they often don't happen.

Major capital projects including those in developing economies will continue to provide opportunities for clean tech innovation. It behoves project developers and their stakeholders to consider clean tech opportunities for both lowering and enhancing the impact of these projects. It is up to governments and regulators to incentivize and absolutely insist on progress in this direction.

Dr Tom Woollard is a principal partner at Environmental Resources Management (ERM) based in London. ERM provides sustainability advice on major capital projects to many of the world's largest oil and gas, power and mining companies.

Further details: tel: 020 3206 5273; e-mail: **tom.woollard@erm.com.**

Nick Cottam writes on business and environmental issues and advises clients on various aspects of corporate communications and marketing.

Further details: mobile: 07834 978139; e-mail: **Nick@nickcottam.com.**

PART THREE
How the market works

Funding future energy

Jeremy Biggs at Narec Capital takes a disruptive view of how to finance innovations in energy technology.

Whilst the debate on the impact of our current energy demands on climate change continues, few are able to deny that the world is facing a growing global energy crisis. As the scale of the challenge unfolds it is likely to produce a requirement for innovation on an unprecedented scale as we aspire to develop alternative sustainable energy solutions, limit our future demand requirements and reduce our reliance on centralized network monopolies. Although the requirement may be evident, many of the companies developing pioneering technologies are facing severe funding gaps as the typical venturing approach struggles to meet the challenges of this emerging sector. Thought must be given to how we can create a new, sustainable approach to funding innovative energy technologies within a structure that optimizes the risk versus reward ratio for early stage investors.

It would appear that despite the scale of the opportunity before us, investors have found it nearly impossible to pick promising technologies that match their risk and return parameters. The sector is often heavily capital-intensive, open to extreme swings in government policy and driven by the requirements of large industrial players. Venture funds typically lack both the skill and the will to invest confidently in this sector and hence choose to shy away until more predictable returns can be evidenced. Whilst some may consider this approach prudent, it is also prone to missing an immense amount of value. To extract value whilst minimizing investment risk, future venture funds must possess an in-depth understanding of the market need and commercial application for the technology, they must align themselves with multiple industrial partners to assess the market demand and implement a robust process for accelerating chosen technologies through to commercialization. Working closely with public-sector funding initiatives and integrating insurance arrangements will also provide additional layers of risk mitigation for early stage investment. The scarcity of early-stage capital means that good value investments can be found, if a venture team have the capability and domain expertise to nurture them safely through to commercialization.

For early stage venturing to happen effectively financiers can no longer sit in isolated, city-based offices pontificating on the performance of distant companies listed on spreadsheets. There is a new role to be played in leading a collaboration of entities whose sole objective is to facilitate the commercial introduction of new technologies to the market. Efforts must focus on creating an entire ecosystem for the commercialization of emerging technologies. Venture funds must understand the integral components of the target technologies' industrial value chain, be able to assimilate and articulate the issues of each component and optimize appropriate solutions for the end client. Only by aligning its funding approach with the strategy of key industrial partners will a fund be able to make informed investment decisions, control the commercialization process and manage early exit strategies for its future portfolio companies.

Forming a collaboration of industrial partners is the key ingredient for early-stage funding success. Many venture funds in this sector have already created a partnership with a leading utility, however this normally only serves to make the fund hostage to a single-investor strategy. Similarly, some utilities have created internal corporate venture capital units, although many have struggled to realize their full potential, as venturing is not deemed a core activity of the business. Far more value can be achieved by aligning a venture fund alongside multiple industrial parties, not as investors but as interested parties. This provides the fund with a balanced view of the market and creates a broad, demand-led environment for promising technologies to be accelerated through to commercialization. The utilities benefit from being exposed to a more diversified product range and sharing early-stage adoption risk with their competitors. It also serves to stimulate the supply chain and creates exit strategies for the fund, as companies look to 'buy in' to the technologies in order to sell effectively to their utility clients. Most utilities will openly admit that they would prefer to buy from a large supply chain partner than an entrepreneur.

Investment risk can also be mitigated by integrating with public-sector funding initiatives and insurance arrangements. Energy and innovation are key areas for public support and as such there are many funding initiatives that can be used to 'match' private funding schemes, where public investment is unlocked by the provision of an element of private capital. Often these funds are underspent as the companies that apply struggle to find the private funding match. At the same time, the public sector is not necessarily incentivized to picking commercial 'winners' and requires experienced investors to lead the way. A fund that can work in conjunction with these initiatives can provide leverage to private capital, often on a one-for-one basis.

Understanding how a technology can impact the end-developers' or operators' insurance is a key element to ensuring that the technology is adopted by its intended market. By their very nature, technologies that intend to disrupt processes will often inadvertently invalidate the insurance of the underlying operation or pose significant additional cost. As an example the average cost of insurance for an offshore wind farm is 26 per cent of OPEX (operating expenditure), mainly due to the risk involved from unproven technologies and methodologies being utilized. The rising cost of project insurance is impacting the propensity of developers to adopt new technologies. Introducing insurance underwriters at an early stage will help to determine whether the technology can be insured itself and identify any likely impact it may have on the operators' insurance policy. This can help to reduce insurance cost and mitigate barriers to entry for the new technology. Often insurers will require an experienced partner to help them understand the various dynamics of the technology in order to write cost-effective policies. The combination of insurance and public funding support can provide a significant risk-reduction effect for an early stage investment.

Dynamic changes in utilities' global business models will produce substantial scope for finding attractive clean technology investments. Public policy and regulation is starting to impact the centralized generation model for utilities. The cost of maintaining centralized infrastructure breaks down as fewer customers pay to utilize the network as they move to produce their own electricity in an effort to avoid rising energy bills. Last year RWE blamed renewable energy sources and the move to decentralized generation (DG) for its lacklustre annual results. It has now adapted its business model to help customers manage and integrate renewable energy rather than invest in centralized generation. The US electric utilities industry group, Edison

Electric Institute, recently identified DG as the largest disruptive threat to utilities business models and financial health as their customer base becomes more and more self-reliant. The more forward-thinking utilities are already starting to work out where they can derive future value by using their scale and access to centralized networks, but will require a host of new technologies to facilitate this move if they want to maintain a competitive advantage. Localized energy storage solutions, grid reliability technologies and community generation schemes will all be key areas of growing future demand for utilities.

Similarly, whilst solving utility problems there will be a great deal of innovation required on the consumer side. Accelerated by rocketing energy bills and an increased awareness of sustainability, more consumers are becoming motivated to change their lifestyles. Passive houses (or houses that produce net zero energy requirements) are now becoming a commercial reality. An emerging UK technology and design company have produced prefabricated houses that comply with Level 6 of the Code for Sustainable Homes as standard. With a predicted rise in household fuel bills of 40 per cent by 2030, these houses will save consumers from their reliance on energy purchased from centralized networks, whilst enabling them to benefit from the revenue streams associated with net energy production and government support mechanisms.

It is unlikely that we will rid ourselves of the requirement for fossil fuels for some time although efforts are being made to reduce consumption. BHP Billiton CEO (Andrew Mackenzie) suggested at a recent US conference that more than 70 per cent of the world's energy will continue to come from fossil fuels until 2030. Whilst one of the world's largest fossil fuel producers would be expected to say this, other more independent sources are predicting anywhere between 40–76 per cent. Integrating biomass alongside coal for incineration, or co-firing, is one way that large power stations such as Drax are looking to reduce their reliance on fossil fuels. However, the addition of biomass into the co-firing process is still extremely inefficient. Burning at different temperatures, differing calorific values, safe storage and logistics all impact on the cost and efficiency of power production. A new technology is now reaching commercialization that can dry both biomass and low-rank coals to produce a product that will burn at consistent temperatures, enable safe storage and reduce the logistics costs from transporting wet feedstock. This new technology can enhance the calorific value by up to 80 per cent, reduce CO_2 emissions and make co-firing a more viable process for power producers to consider, thereby helping to reduce our over-all consumption of fossil fuel.

Great change is upon us as the global energy industry looks to adapt its future business model to balance increasing consumer demand with more sustainable sources of power generation. Further decentralization of the grid will see utilities moving towards a service provision model as they struggle to hold onto an increasingly mobile customer base. The need for innovation to enable this change to occur is growing increasingly acute and significant investment opportunities can be harvested by those who are willing to take a different approach to standard venturing models. Leading a collaborative effort between multiple industrial partners that are aligned but not integral to the investment manager, implementing a robust commercialization process, integrating with public-sector funding initiatives and insurance partners will be the only way to identify real opportunity and manage the inherent risk of early stage investment. Although there will be plenty of disruptive technologies to choose from, it will be a new disruptive approach to funding that will enable investors to capture the true value of this emerging sustainable energy sector.

Jeremy Biggs is the CEO of Narec Capital, a joint venture between The National Renewable Energy Centre (Narec) and Ashberg Ltd, a fully regulated financial services entity. Narec Capital is the UK's renewable energy accelerator, a public/private initiative established to leverage Narec's unique test asset base in order to de-risk and provide finance for renewable technologies and projects.

Jeremy is also a Founding Director of Ashberg Ltd, which focuses on direct private investments primarily in the areas of renewable energy and sustainability. Jeremy has over 10 years' experience of banking and investment management. He regularly speaks on clean technology investment and the role of private finance.

Further information is available from Jeremy Biggs (tel: 020 3036 0440; e-mail: **jbiggs@nareccapital.com**; website: **www.nareccapital.com**).

The value of measuring carbon

Melanie Eddis and **Nick Cottam** discuss carbon measurement, reporting and assurance as a driver of clean tech innovation and performance.

Business cares about carbon. This is still evident in a post-economic crash global economy, as companies from a range of sectors claim that responding to the threat of climate change is now ingrained in the way they operate.

Why should this be so? Why do large companies, many of them in high-impact sectors but some with much lighter footprints, still care about their greenhouse gas (GHG) emissions? The answer, it seems, is a combination of pressure from a range of stakeholders; reputation (not least to achieve a good 'score' from investment ratings); national requirements such as the UK mandatory GHG reporting regulation; and the business benefits achieved from energy efficiency and innovation delivered by clean(er) tech products and processes.

CDP as a reporting driver

Whatever the drivers, a company needs a baseline against which to monitor the efficiency of clean tech investment. This involves measuring the appropriate indicator, be it megawatts, miles, or litres, and calculating the GHG emissions using an accepted methodology such as the GHG Protocol. Annual monitoring and reporting using this consistent approach allows both management and stakeholders to see the progress made and take decisions accordingly.

Integrating carbon into business goals as a response to the climate change issue is not going to go away. For its part the CDP (formerly the Carbon Disclosure Project) – now covering both carbon and water use – requested information from some 11,000 organizations globally in 2013, an increase of 37 per cent on the previous year. The onus on all CDP reporters is to provide accurate and credible information as a very public indication of their performance in these areas. As noted below, they also get credit for demonstrating third-party assurance.

In terms of direct audience, the CDP represents more than 650 institutional investors, who are either signatories to demonstrate their support for the project or who provide funding as CDP members. Between them, these investors have a combined US $78 trillion under management. In 2013, CDP's third annual Carbon Action (CA) report headlined the fact that GHG reduction initiatives across different sectors are continuing to generate a return on investment (ROI) of 33 per cent, which the CA report suggests has created US $15 billion in value. From a company standpoint, measuring, reporting and assurance are an important part of a process to give management confidence in the information needed to make clean tech investment decisions.

Clean tech innovation, whether we are talking about changes to a building's fabric or more energy-efficient products and processes, can be driven both by the big sticks of being seen to do nothing and failing to prepare for the future and by the carrots of reduced operating costs and enhanced reputation. The end-of-life mine that creates a pump-and-treat system to generate hydroelectricity is being clever about its legacy but is also likely to win praise from different stakeholder groups. Elimination of visible emission sources such as flares is likely to secure support from communities living close to oil and gas facilities as well as reducing wastage of precious energy resources.

Building on the old adage that you can't manage without measuring, the process of carbon footprinting has enabled companies to set ambitious carbon reduction targets before seeking assurance on methodologies and data and reporting the results via CDP and other media such as the annual report. The same applies to water footprinting as companies seek to manage consumption of a scarce resource more carefully – and demonstrate that they are doing so. The result – aside from meeting the requirements of organizations such as CDP – will include more informed energy/resource management and better decision-making around those resources.

Third-party assurance

Although not mandatory, CDP asks for disclosure on whether the disclosed GHG inventory has been verified according to defined standards listed on its website. Companies able to demonstrate that such assurance has been satisfactorily completed are awarded additional 'points' and can enhance their standing compared with others in their sector.

These same companies know that good quality GHG data is an important aid to decision-making, and effective third-party assurance provides not only the much-needed confidence but also fresh insights into where improvements can be made. Enhanced focus on GHG reporting forces a company to look at how it uses energy and materials and opens the door to innovative solutions that can change the ways employees work, buildings are designed or goods are made. This is as true for the mining company that developed a small wind farm near the site of a tailings facility as it is for a supermarket, such as Tesco, which has extended its GHG measurement across its carbon footprint and has sought to engage its customers through selective carbon labelling.

Office-based businesses also have great potential, as Deutsche Bank demonstrated when it chose to renovate a pair of 30-year-old towers in Frankfurt, implementing many innovative and progressive techniques. As a result, the bank claims to have cut down on its energy supply by a half, water consumption by over 70 per cent and CO_2 emissions by almost 90 per cent, making the new towers – awarded the highest possible certifications of LEED (Leadership in Energy Efficient Design): Platinum and DGNB (translates to German Sustainable Building Council): Gold – one of the most eco-friendly high-rise buildings in the world.

Deutsche Bank has secured independent assurance on its GHG and other environmental data from ERM CVS since 2008. Ottmar Kayser, Director with responsibility for sustainability-related management processes said:

> The assurance process opened our eyes to some of the limitations of our data collection processes and led us to invest in data management systems that enhanced our ability to track our performance and take informed steps to achieve our sustainability goals. One of these goals was the carbon-neutrality of our global business operations by the end of 2012.

The drive for clean tech innovation is relevant to different business sectors and for a number of technologies, from Heat Exchange Units and Economizers for waste heat recovery to the new generation of energy efficient boilers. Companies getting a better understanding of their energy consumption and carbon emissions have every incentive to find new ways to reduce on both counts.

Material risks

Investors who support CDP also believe that GHG emissions continue to be a material risk across a range of sectors. This is evident, for example, in the comments investors make with regard to CDP and reputational/licence to operate issues and the efforts of CDP reporting companies to seek out clean tech investments – for example, renewable energy sources and more energy efficient product development – which will help to reduce GHG emissions in the medium and long term. Companies that continue to manage and report on GHG emissions and energy consumption are demonstrating effective risk management in addition to the already noted innovation.

The authors' professional understanding of assurance is that it should be more than a box-ticking exercise, whether the assurer is certifying to a management system such as ISO 14001 or looking at a specific data set such as those relating to GHG emissions for CDP. While in the latter example assurance seeks to verify the data, it should also be examining the processes for gathering that data which in turn helps to set future targets and drive performance. A good assurance provider will evaluate the efficiency and robustness of processes and internal controls as well as check that the data are calculated correctly, which helps a company to embed a focus on the metrics that matter across the organization.

Another key challenge for businesses that seek to drive down GHG emissions is getting the support of their supply chains. According to a 2013 survey report *Collaborative Action on Climate Risk*, written by Accenture on behalf of the CDP, investment in low-carbon projects is falling from 2012 and 2011 levels. Smaller companies, it seems, need a stronger incentive to invest these days – for example gains in energy efficiency through clean tech innovation or indeed the encouragement of changing consumer behaviour.

Consumer behaviour

The Accenture survey report noted that 56 per cent of companies identifying climate change-related opportunities say that their customers are becoming more receptive to low-carbon products and services, while 85 per cent of those suppliers surveyed say that consumer behaviour is already changing or will do so in the next one to five years. These respondents identified changing consumer behaviour as the biggest opportunity from climate change.

Consumer behaviour would appear to be a factor to watch at the time of writing this chapter. On the one hand consumers in the UK and other European countries face steeply rising energy costs, both for the goods and services in the home and in other areas such as transport. Many of these same consumers are also on the receiving end of what appears to be a rising tide of extreme weather events. Favouring companies that are seen to reduce their GHG emissions, likely in the future to be embodied in clearly visible product labels as well as corporate reports, will indeed be another aspect of consumer behaviour and consumer choice.

Melanie Eddis is the partner in charge of climate change services with ERM Certification and Verification Services (ERM CVS), the global environment, health and safety, certification and verification business of the ERM Group, one of the world's largest providers of professional sustainability and EHS services. ERM CVS delivers both external and internal corporate and facility-level assurance and verification in relation to sustainability reporting, GHG emissions and other EHS and sustainability performance data across a range of voluntary and compliance schemes.

Further details: tel: 020 8458 5679; e-mail: **melanie.eddis@ermcvs.com**; website: **www.ermcvs.com**.

Nick Cottam writes on business and environmental issues and advises clients on various aspects of corporate communications and marketing.

Further details: mobile: 07834 978139; e-mail: **Nick@nickcottam.com**.

Structuring techniques for demand-side management solutions

You have a strategic objective for going green and modifying your demand for energy, but what structuring techniques can you use to set up and implement demand-side management solutions, asks **Michael Rudd** at Bird & Bird.

An energy consumer wishes to implement a holistic demand-side management strategy that will include a broad range of solutions including an energy performance contract, decentralized generation and demand-side response technologies, as well as procure and manage an off-site power purchase agreement and flexible energy supply contracts. As it has limited internal demand-side management expertise and only wishes to dedicate part of its financial resources to implementing the strategy, the energy consumer wishes to select (through a competitive tender process) an energy services company (ESCO) to deliver the solutions. A substantive part of the ESCO's funding for the solutions is likely to come from third-party debt and equity funding.

When the transaction is presented to the energy consumer's decision-makers for final approval, the project team leading the transaction will want to do so with confidence that they will receive approval to enter into the transaction. An important part of that confidence comes from knowing that the transaction has appropriately addressed key issues, such as ownership of the relevant assets and various financial matters. This requires appropriate decision-making tools that ensure all relevant considerations are taken into account at the relevant decision-making points.

Demand-side management: an overview

Demand-side management encompasses a range of activities designed to modify consumer demand for energy. It reflects a growing strategic trend within many organizations and can include a range of solutions such as the following (with the potential benefits outlined in Table 3.3.1):

- *Energy performance contracts*: a contractual arrangement between the beneficiary and the provider of an energy efficiency improvement measure (eg ESCO), verified and monitored during the whole contractual term, where investments (work, supply or service) in that measure are paid for in relation to a contractually agreed level of energy efficiency improvement or other agreed energy performance criterion, such as financial savings.[1]

- *Decentralized generation*: the supply of heat, cooling and/or electricity generated on or proximate to the end-consumer's site, utilizing a renewable source and/or an efficient form of generation (eg combined heat and power).

- *Demand-side response*: this involves either a temporary reduction in, or a shift in the time of use of, power by consumers.[2] Traditionally only available to large (eg industrial) consumers, in some countries, a combination of government policy, innovative new market entrants (such as aggregators) and technologies (such as voltage optimization) has opened this market up to smaller energy consumers.

- *Off-site power purchase agreements*: the purchase of electricity by a consumer directly from renewable generators not on or proximate to their site. For example, a large energy consumer buying wind power in one country to provide renewable power to their operations in a neighbouring country.

- *Flexible energy supply contract*: a type of supply contract utilized by larger energy consumers which gives the consumer flexibility by allowing it to set and reset the price now for energy it will consume

TABLE 3.3.1 Demand-side management solutions and potential benefits

Demand-side management solution	Has the potential to…					
	Reduce energy consumption	Reduce energy costs	Generate income	Improve security of supply	Reduce carbon footprint	Achieve renewable targets
Energy performance contracts	x	x	x		x	x
Decentralized generation		x	x	x	x	x
Demand-side response	x		x		x	
Off-site power purchase agreements		x	x	x	x	x
Flexible energy supply contract	x	x	x		x	x

in future periods (eg if the consumer thinks energy prices are going up, they may want to set now the price for supplies in future periods).

Key issues

Managing the process

A carefully managed process requires consideration of the key issues such as ownership and financial matters at various points during the process. This may include:

- by the energy consumer prior to commencing the procurement process. This enables it to determine its ideal position on each of the key issues as well as the extent it permits ESCO bidders to submit variations to the ideal position;
- by the ESCO in preparing and submitting its tender, including the extent to which its tender deviates from the energy consumer's ideal position;
- by the energy consumer when evaluating each ESCO's tender, including the extent it will deviate from its ideal position in selecting its preferred ESCO bidder;
- following selection of the preferred ESCO bidder and during any subsequent negotiations leading up to the entry into the relevant contracts and financial close.

Ownership

The question seems straightforward – Who will own the assets required to deliver the demand-side management solutions? Sometimes the answer is also straightforward. However, sometimes the answer is more nuanced because of the relevant considerations below. It is also important to remember the distinction between legal ownership (title) versus other interests in the asset. For example, if the ESCO does not own an asset (even though it is responsible for the funding, design and build of such asset) due to property law then it may be able to have legal possession of the assets through appropriate leasing arrangements. The ESCO and its funders may require this because it enables the ESCO to directly claim a fiscal incentive that underpins financial viability of the project for the ESCO and its funders.

To enable the energy consumer's project team to come to an informed decision on ownership, it is recommended that they consider the following:

- Which entity will own the assets? In addition to considering this from the perspective of each of the key stakeholders, the stakeholders will also need to consider whether to utilize an existing entity or establish a new transaction-specific entity. The energy consumer is considering allocating part of its financial resources to implementing its strategy. One way it could achieve this is establishing an incorporated or unincorporated joint venture entity with the ESCO in which the energy consumer invests an agreed amount into the joint venture.

- Are there any commercial, legal or technical barriers to achieving the ideal ownership structure? These may include:

  - **Commercial:**
    - Financial arrangements: as outlined in more detail below, particularly the preferred accounting treatment (for example, the energy consumer may want the assets to sit off its balance sheet) and the fiscal incentives available which may only allow the person owning the assets to claim the fiscal incentive. Corporate policy requirements: for example, it is possible that the selected ESCO's corporate policy is that it must own the assets if it is responsible for funding the capital costs.
    - Third-party funder requirements: although there are alternative transactional structures which a third-party funder will accept, the usual preference for a third-party funder is that the borrower (eg the ESCO) should own the assets.

  - **Legal:**
    - Statute dealing with asset ownership – for example, if the energy consumer is a strategically important public body (eg in the defence sector) then statute may require that all the assets are owned by the public body.
    - Property law – in many jurisdictions property law may influence ownership. For example, in the UK an asset may be considered a fixture depending upon the degree, purpose and intention of affixation. This could lead to some or all of the assets financed, designed and installed by an ESCO being owned by the energy consumer if they are affixed to the energy consumer's property.

— Existing commercial/contractual arrangements – existing
arrangements may influence the ownership arrangements.
The energy consumer may have an existing arrangement with
a facilities management company and/or have relevant
insurances in place that covers the assets where it makes
commercial sense (eg more cost-effective) for the energy
consumer to own some or all of the assets.

- Technical:

— Integration – are the assets integrated into existing infrastructure
which, in addition to any property law considerations, makes
separate legal ownership more difficult from a technical
perspective, such as it being technically challenging to separate
the operation and maintenance of those assets from the existing
infrastructure?

— Essential assets: are the assets essential to a stakeholder's other
activities? The energy consumer may require ownership of
certain assets because if the ESCO owned such assets and
subsequently went insolvent then the energy consumer's
business could be significantly disrupted.

- Is the person who owns different from the person who uses or is in
possession of the assets? For example:

  - The energy consumer may be the primary user of some of the assets
such as energy efficient lighting installed by the ESCO.

  - As outlined above, the ESCO may require legal possession of some
of the assets even if it does not have legal ownership which could be
granted through appropriate leasing arrangements.

- What happens on expiry or early termination? Assuming ESCO is
responsible for the design and build of the relevant assets, does the
ESCO:

  - remove any of the assets on expiry or early termination; or

  - transfer ownership of the assets to the energy consumer? If so:

    — Is this automatic, at the election of one party or by agreement?

    — What payment(s) must the energy consumer make to the
ESCO? This could include a payment for the ESCO's lost

future income stream that it would have derived from the
assets (in the case of early termination typically calculated on
a net present value basis) and/or a payment for the fair market
value of the assets.

For example, if the term of the contract between the energy consumer and
the ESCO covers a predominant part of the economic life of the assets then
on expiry it may be appropriate for ESCO to remove the asset but on early
termination there should be an appropriate mechanism to enable the transfer
ownership of the assets to the energy consumer.

Financial matters

Like ownership, the financial matters relevant to implementing a transaction
can be straightforward or complex. The complexity often arises in the green
economy because of fiscal 'sticks and carrots' that exist to stimulate behavioural change.

To enable the energy consumer's project team to come to an informed
decision on ownership, it is recommended that they consider the following:

- Who funds the capital expenditure for the assets required to deliver
  the demand-side management solutions? The ESCO is likely to fund
  the majority of the capital expenditure on the basis it will directly or
  indirectly recover it through the income streams referred to below.
  The energy consumer may:

  - potentially contribute to the capital expenditure typically for a
    financial return such as entitlement to retain a greater percentage
    of the energy savings or a cheaper energy supply tariff for the
    on-site generation;

  - be responsible to contribute (in whole or part) to any additional
    capital expenditure caused by it, such as variations initiated by it
    during the construction phase or specific risks which have been
    allocated to it (eg delays caused by the energy consumer).

- Who funds the operational expenditure for the assets required to
  deliver the demand-side management solutions? Once again, the ESCO
  is likely to bear the operational expenditure on the basis it will directly
  or indirectly recover it through the income streams referred to below.

- What income streams does the transaction generate for each stakeholder? For example:
  - ESCO's income: the ESCO could potentially receive the following income streams:
    — payments from the energy consumer for:
      - the majority of the energy savings achieved from the assets;
      - the supply of energy generated from an on-site or off-site generation facility;
      - services provided by ESCO to the energy consumer, such as managing the energy consumer's flexible energy supply contract(s).
    — sale of energy to third parties, such as the export of electricity from the on-site generation to the grid under a power purchase agreement;
    — payments (eg from the grid operator) for the provision of demand-side response services;
    — fiscal incentives.
  - Energy consumer's income: the energy consumer could potentially receive the following income streams:
    — payments from the ESCO for:
      - property-lease rental relating to any property lease granted by the energy consumer to the ESCO (eg for the on-site generation system);
      - equipment-lease rental relating to any assets owned by the energy consumer. This could be relevant if the energy consumer funds the installation of specific assets, owns such assets and grants an equipment lease to ESCO to enable it to have legal possession.
    — a share of the energy savings achieved from the assets;
    — a share of income from the provision of demand-side response services;
    — fiscal incentives to the extent not claimed by the ESCO.

- The energy consumer and the ESCO will need to agree the payment mechanics including any initial payment amounts and how any amounts are adjusted. For example, in relation to energy saving payments, the parties will need to agree the baseline energy consumption and the periodic measurement and verification process (eg based on the International Performance Measurement and Verification Protocol) to determine the actual energy savings achieved.

- On whose balance sheet does the asset sit? Balance sheet treatment depends upon a number of factors, including the risk distribution. Risk is transferred from one party to another (eg from the energy consumer to the ESCO) where it faces sufficient financial consequences. The key risks are finance, construction, performance, availability, operation and maintenance, demand and the long-term risk and reward of ownership. A key challenge in many transactions is that risks are allocated between a number of parties. This diversity requires a case-by-case analysis of risk in a variety of scenarios (perhaps using Monte Carlo simulations) in which the transaction characteristics are considered as a whole to determine where the balance of risk lies and whether it should be on or off a party's balance sheet.

There are, of course, other important considerations, including additional tax and accounting issues as well as credit risk and funder's security requirements.

Conclusion

The diversity between organizations and their green economy strategies means there is no 'one-size-fits-all' implementation solution. A common theme to the 'success stories' is a well-managed process that utilizes decision-making tools in which the above and other relevant issues (including ensuring all of the transaction risks are allocated, mitigated and managed) are taken into account at the relevant decision-making points. As organizations learn from previous success stories in implementing their own strategies and share their own success stories, a virtuous circle is created. This leads to the establishment of best practice and commoditization; both essential elements to the long-term growth of the demand-side management market.

Michael Rudd is a commercial projects and regulatory partner who specializes in innovations within the energy and utilities sector, with a particular focus on the built environment. He has advised investors, green companies and public and private sector energy consumers and property developers looking for demand-side management solutions including projects that have won industry innovation awards. He is editor of a renewables book and contributed to a variety of other books and industry papers. He is a Member of the Institute of Directors and a Fellow of the Royal Society of Arts.

Further details: tel: + 44 (0)20 7415 6174; e-mail: **michael.rudd@twobirds.com**; website: **www.twobirds.com**.

Notes

1 Directive 2012/27/EU of the European Parliament and of the Council of 25 October 2012 on energy efficiency, amending Directives 2009/125/EC and 2010/30/EU and repealing Directives 2004/8/EC and 2006/32/EC [2012] (OJ L315, 12.11.2012) Art 2 (27).

2 Smart Grid GB and Bird & Bird LLP, Energy Bill 2013: Demand-side response and the capacity market in focus, *Smart Grid GB*, August 2013, 9, [Online] http://www.smartgridgb.org/policy-regulation/item/293-sggb-releases-new-report-on-capacity-market-and-dsr.html.

Responsibly sourced

Actively manage your supply chain to build a clean reputation,

says **Ian Nicholson** at Responsible Solutions.

Sustainability is usually defined as delivering the triple bottom line of minimizing environmental impact whilst achieving social equity and economic success. These topics have become relatively mainstream and are talked about in most organizations within the built environment sector on a daily basis. However, much of the focus of these discussions tends to be about managing environmental issues and, in particular, reducing carbon emissions. Indeed, for many, being sustainable only means being low-carbon or even carbon-neutral. Due to the vast range of environmental legislation in place many organizations are also well advanced in their consideration of waste management, resource efficiency, pollution prevention, water management and ecological issues. But even with these wider issues included, this is still only really focusing on the environmental aspect of the triple bottom line.

It is plausible to suggest that many companies focus more on their environmental impacts due to heightened public awareness. For example, publicizing product- and organizational-level carbon footprints has, in recent years, become common practice across a multitude of industries in response to increased awareness of the carbon agenda and how it contributes to climate change. Essentially, this is due to the organization's perception of risk, and what it considers high- and low-risk issues. As the whole topic of climate change and carbon has gained such wide public awareness, it is much more likely that an organization will identify it as a high-risk issue affecting the business.

ResponsibleSolutions

Helping you profit from a cleaner corporate **conscience**

STRATEGY AND SYSTEMS
Environmental Management Systems; Health and Safety Management Systems; Business Processes; Virtual Environment Manager; Corporate Responsibility Strategies; Sustainable Procurement Strategies

SUPPLY CHAIN RESPONSIBILITY
Responsible Sourcing; Supplier Management; Data Collection and Analysis

TRAINING
Environmental Awareness; Supply Chains; Sales Force; Face-to-Face; e-Learning

REPORTING AND COMMUNICATIONS
Marketing Materials; Performance Reports; Environmental Labels and Declarations; Carbon Footprint; Life Cycle Analysis; Verification

www.responsible-solutions.co.uk
Tel: 01509 320100
Email: info@responsible-solutions.co.uk

In practice, nowadays the majority of organizations incorporate environmental initiatives into their day-to-day operations. As a result some organizations, particularly larger, publically owned companies, have expanded their activities beyond environmental matters and have begun to consider corporate social responsibility (CSR), the first step of which expands environmental performance into looking at giving something back to the communities in which the organization is operating. Typically, this covers philanthropic issues, such as being a good neighbour and allowing employees to undertake volunteering activities within their communities. However, this should only be the starting point for social considerations as there are potentially many risks, both environmental and social, to reputation within the supply chain. For instance, ensuring fair labour practices and standards of working and living for employees is something that in the UK is almost a given for any organization.

However, due to the international nature of supply chains the question must be asked: How aware are you of such social issues within those supplier companies that are not based within the UK? Maintaining high social standards therefore holds as much importance from a risk perspective for an organization as environmental initiatives such as waste or carbon, but do organizations actively audit suppliers on such issues when making purchasing decisions, for example?

This is slowly beginning to change within the built environment sector and some organizations are starting to realize that their sustainability strategies and performance need to demonstrate understanding of what is occurring within the whole supply chain. So, how well do you know what is going on within your supply chain? To come to an initial assessment, try asking the following three questions of your organization:

1 Are all the raw materials in our product traceable back to the source of each raw material?

2 Are we aware of the performance of all the companies within our supply chain with regard to environmental, ethical and health and safety performance?

3 Are we aware of how our brand is perceived in the business world, by our customers and perhaps by the public at large?

If you are answering no to any of these questions, then there are potential risks to the reputation of your business.

Case studies of reputation

Some industry sectors have been considering this for some time, so let's have a brief look at some examples:

- *Nike*: The sportswear and apparel manufacturer was exposed in the mid-1990s for use of child labour and sweatshops in Asian manufacturing sites. Aside from the public embarrassment of being linked with such damaging stories, consumer boycotts of Nike products led to reports of a fall in sales of around 8 per cent and decline in share value of 15 per cent. Nike-branded apparel is popular on a global scale and linking manufacture of Nike products with unethical treatment of workers and low levels of pay can cause consumers to deem ownership of such apparel as a statement of support or lack of care for such situations, causing them to source their products from alternative companies to avoid being linked with such unethical practices.

- *Primark*: The clothing retailer was exposed in the UK press as recently as 2009 for alleged use of illegal immigrants and poor working conditions at one of its UK suppliers. Similar to Nike, the publicity associated with such actions led to consumer boycotts, and once Primark were associated with a poor reputation among consumers, it proved difficult to change this stance.

- *Coltan and cassiterite*: These two metals are used in the production of mobile phones and other electronic products. A recent documentary looked at the human rights and ethical issues associated with the mining of these metals in the Democratic Republic of Congo (DRC), which owns around 80 per cent of global reserves. Ownership of a mobile phone, and sustained consumer demand for the latest upgrades and models is funding a war in the DRC – an issue that should resonate with the vast majority of consumers, given that most people now own a mobile phone. There is currently relatively low awareness around these 'conflict minerals' however, and, unlike the case with Nike, it is unlikely that mobile phone companies will see a fall in consumer demand for new mobile phones. Worryingly, the documentary found little evidence that mobile phone companies were taking any action.

- *Dow Chemical*: The selection of Dow Chemical as the supplier of the fabric wrap around the Olympic Stadium for the London 2012 Olympic Games became the subject of intense opposition and protest from a number of parties, and even led to the Indian team threatening to withdraw from the Games altogether. The reason for such opposition was that Dow had purchased Union Carbide, which operated the Bhopal plant – the location of a devastating industrial accident in 1984, and their subsequent non-payment of compensation to victims of the disaster created a highly negative reputation for both the organization and its products.

These examples show that reputation is key and should possibly, for many organizations, be classified as a higher risk than carbon. They also demonstrate that transparency is important; an open, honest approach to how a company conducts its operations is more likely to resonate positively with society.

Early steps in the construction industry

Within the built environment and construction supply chains, awareness of such ethical and social concerns is low due to it being a relatively new concept in this arena. However many raw construction materials, such as natural stone or sand, are often sourced from quarries located in countries such as India and China, where human rights and ethical issues are not subject to such intense scrutiny as in the West. Recently for example, a major UK natural stone supplier discovered on a routine visit to supplier sites in Asia that young children were actively employed on site – a serious problem in itself, yet to exacerbate the issue it was then discovered that access to personal protective equipment (PPE) was lacking. In this case, the company opted to work with local agencies to raise awareness about these issues and to provide new PPE, while eliminating child labour on all sites. The company in question here recognized that active management of their supply chain was the only means by which they could guarantee that their materials and products were sourced, while observing satisfactory ethical and social requirements. However, it would have been much easier, although perhaps less morally palatable, for that particular company to simply walk away from the situation, opting instead to source its materials from elsewhere.

This introduces another dimension to the issue of ethics; while quarry conditions were clearly in need of improvement, without the UK company's custom, the supplier would suffer impacts to business, which could cause workers to suffer loss of employment. Indeed, Primark terminated business with many such suppliers when they discovered issues of child labour in their supply chain – a move that became the subject of heavy criticism from some groups who felt this may cause additional hardship for the workers and children. Although in developed countries, working conditions such as these would be deemed unethical, in many developing countries where poverty is commonplace, working in such conditions is actually preferable as it still provides a basic income that keeps people out of poverty. This suggests that pro-active supply chain management is far more preferable, and simply dis-associating oneself from such supply chains may not necessarily be the most appropriate thing to do.

Responsible sourcing in building services and M&E – the next steps

Staying with the construction industry, a sector where recent progress in this area has been encouraging, the first standards specific to construction products now have some purchase within the industry, with a number of construction product manufacturing companies working towards certification to evidence proactivity with regard to ethics in the supply chain. However, these standards only appeared in 2009 in the form of the Building Research Establishment (BRE) BES 6001 standard and BS 8902 from BSi for responsible sourcing schemes, and so there is still a long way to go. Currently, take-up of these standards has focused on core construction materials and products such as aggregates, cement, concrete, bricks, steel, gypsum and glass.

This is only scratching the surface – many products that often represent high proportions of a construction project's value currently cannot be certified under such schemes. For example, mechanical and electrical (M&E) components such as lighting, heating and ventilation system products are not currently being certified and some are questioning whether the current standards are appropriate for certifying such products. This is beginning to create issues for clients wanting to classify their building as 'responsibly sourced';

M&E can typically represent around 40 per cent of a building's components and so clearly there is a substantial mass of materials that are not yet able to demonstrate traceability issues for their supply chains in a standardized way. Currently, the industry is striving for this next step and progress is beginning to be made through the APRES programme (**http://apres.lboro.ac.uk/**).

The built environment sector isn't unique in this slow start, the coltan example in mobile phones discussed earlier demonstrates that the whole of the technology sector is still getting to grips with this issue and has a long way to go. The technology boom has created increased demand for these metals resulting in their value soaring. The continued purchasing of these 'conflict minerals' is financing a civil war – the bloodiest conflict since World War II, according to some human rights organizations (see the documentary Blood in the Mobile, **http://bloodinthemobile.org**, 2004). This war is unlikely to cease unless demand for these metals halts – armed groups are able to finance the war by selling off these minerals to mobile phone manufacturers. Material traceability comes back into question here – a documentary that looked into the supply of cassiterite showed that, of the mobile phone manufacturers that were interviewed, none of them could guarantee that they were not sourcing cassiterite from the Congo.

In the construction industry there is some evidence of change: Crossrail, one of the largest and most significant infrastructure projects ever undertaken within the UK is taking a very proactive approach with regard to implementing ethical concerns into their procurement policies. Responsible procurement and ethical behaviour are both identified as key sustainability drivers; and the development of social audit criteria and matrices for assessing high- and low-risk materials including M&E products, with specific focus on country of origin, are evidence that social and ethical considerations are being integrated into all of Crossrail's procurement decisions.

Conclusions

So while carbon and resource efficiency are important, aspects of sustainability and investment must continue in these areas. It is important that clean technology and clean profits consider the wider issues of sustainability; it would surely not be considered ethical if clean technology was delivered at the expense of social equity. As a result, the implementation of CSR has to go beyond the philanthropic activities and consider the much higher reputational risks of ethical issues within supply chains. As mentioned earlier, the starting point is to trace products back to the source of each raw material; from there it is possible to start to identify and manage the issues which will form an important step in creating a clean reputation for your business.

Ian Nicholson is Managing Director of Responsible Solutions Ltd (website: **www.responsible-solutions.co.uk**) and has an MSc in Responsibility and Business Practice. Responsible Solutions are an environmental and corporate responsibility consultancy providing advice on environmental and corporate responsibility strategies, systems and reporting, employee training, supply chain support, life cycle analysis and environmental product declarations. They are one of the leading consultancies advising the construction industry and its supply chain on responsible sourcing and are a founding member of the APRES network.

The input of Professor Jacqui Glass of Loughborough University and James Upstill-Goddard of Responsible Solutions in writing this chapter is gratefully acknowledged.

Energy system modelling

Modelling the UK energy system is essential for meeting future challenges, argues **George Day**, the Head of Economic Strategy at the Energy Technologies Institute (ETI).

Energy system modelling has been around for almost 30 years, based largely on a tool known as 'Markal' developed initially by the International Energy Agency (IEA). Now used in more than 37 countries, similar models that allow users to explore choices across the electricity, heat, transport, industrial and infrastructure sectors have been used in the UK to inform energy policy reviews in recent years. The adoption of carbon budgets and the creation of the Committee on Climate Change (CCC) have also added further impetus; and the CCC has used energy system modelling (principally Markal-based) to support its work on carbon budgets and pathways to 2050.

The Department for Energy and Climate Change (DECC) has also used Markal and the ETI's own modelling tool ESME (Energy System Modelling Environment), as well as other models, to inform its decision-making on carbon budgets and the UK carbon plan, as well as its carbon capture and storage (CCS) roadmap and strategies on heat and bioenergy.

One of the key early initiatives for the ETI – a public/private partnership between global industries and government – was to build an energy system model to guide priorities for a portfolio of technology development programmes. ESME was conceived to help identify investments in the technologies that can deliver the greatest strategic added value to meeting the UK's carbon reduction objectives. Since then, ESME has developed into one of the UK's most powerful energy system models, widely used by its members and others.

What can modelling tell us?

It is reasonable to ask what energy system modelling can tell us that is relevant to real world decision making. How can energy system models such as ESME help support sound policy-making and investment strategies?

Players in the market may want to use modelling to guide commercial judgements about investments in technology development or market strategy, but for policy-makers, energy system modelling can seem uncomfortably close to a kind of algorithmic winner picking, within a utopia of technological determinism. Those who espouse the power of free markets to deliver efficient outcomes might argue that modelling is akin to crystal-ball gazing.

We need to be cautious about the limits of our present-day knowledge, let alone our computational ability to represent complex real-time technical interactions; or the unfathomable behaviour of human decision-makers within markets of the future.

Models implicitly assume that decision-makers have perfect foresight: a far cry from the real-world conditions for investors and firms in the market place. Modelling inevitably simplifies real-world complexities, political constraints, and imperfect knowledge, so its use in informing policy and investment choices must be tempered with caution and judgement. However, there are characteristics of energy systems that arguably make a systems-modelling approach capable of generating novel insights of value for investors and policy-makers.

The characteristics

Energy systems are complex and governed by well-understood physical laws. This means that quantitative modelling is capable of representing system interactions and capturing dynamics that would otherwise not be understood. The drive to meet carbon targets also makes the different parts of our national energy system more strongly integrated in an economic sense because investments in reducing emissions become substitutable across power, heat, transport and industrial sectors. Physical- and engineering-based modelling of energy systems enables us to understand these interactions and to identify gaps and barriers in current economic and market structures.

Modelling also allows us to explore how different primary sources of energy (such as fossil fuels, nuclear and renewables) and vectors for transmission and distribution can compete and interact to meet consumers' ultimate needs such as electricity, gaseous or liquid fuels and heat (for mobility, or for comfort, light and power).

Energy also relies heavily on networks and the uptake of many potential new technologies will be influenced by 'network effects'. This is where the value or attractiveness of a good or service depends on the extent of its adoption or the creation of a supporting network infrastructure. An example might be the introduction of new transport fuels and technologies, such as electric vehicles, where uptake may depend on a critical mass of users and outlets being reached. Building an 'early lead' may be key to achieving widespread uptake and eventual dominance. In energy markets, this may work through early policy choices around incentives for new technologies. Modelling enables policy-makers and potential investors to explore these issues.

Energy markets

Energy markets are shaped extensively by policy and regulation for a variety of reasons, including policy concerns around externalities such as carbon emissions and planning, market power in monopoly networks and the political economy of energy security and affordability. Energy services also require intervention and agreement to establish appropriate market institutions and conventions to facilitate trading and co-ordination within integrated systems.

Energy system modelling provides a vehicle for examining underlying cost and engineering challenges of meeting consumer needs, in a policy-neutral context. A systems-modelling approach will generate insights that no individual market participant would have an incentive to explore and expose. This modelling, and the insights it exposes, allows policy-makers to understand and analyse how policies, markets and incentives could be aligned to deliver energy systems of the future that reduce emissions cost-effectively.

The scale of investment

The scale of investment and challenge required means that the returns to improving policy and investment choices are likely to be high. Figures for the UK's investment requirements in moving to a low-carbon economy run into the hundreds of billions of pounds. Many of the investments needed are in long-life assets, so the need to take a view far into the future is unavoidable. Right-sizing new assets, designing new networks well and making the right choices in renewing assets – or perhaps avoiding major errors – will reduce the costs of later retro-fitting and extend asset lives. The benefits of marginal improvements to investment and policy choices could dwarf figures typically quoted in impact assessments for many policy or regulatory decisions.

However, users of energy system models need to be aware of the limitations of analysis, and the particular features of individual models. For example, ESME uses simplified representations of cost structures, particularly for technologies that depend on economies of scale or that require lumpy investment in supporting infrastructures, such as treating hydrogen infrastructure as an overhead for hydrogen vehicles.

More difficult limitations relate to the difficulty of representing issues like technology risk, which in the real world, have a direct impact on costs through insurance, transactions costs and the cost and difficulties of financing. Issues around bankability and the development of credible new business models are, in practice, vital in the deployment of new technologies, but are not represented in modelling. System modelling arguably still has a long way to go in understanding and calibrating the treatment of changes in consumer surplus associated with technology performance and consumers' experience.

No energy system model can fully reflect the complex physical reality of a national energy system. Technologies and markets evolve unpredictably, disruptive new technologies emerge and consumers' preferences interact and develop in new ways. Energy system models can fail and even the most sophisticated systems modelling tools are vulnerable to major policy mistakes and inflexibility. In the UK we are only at the start of using systems modelling to inform pragmatic policy-making. However, it is a role that will increase over time, with increasingly sophisticated modelling tools being used and developed to inform decisions about the energy systems of the future.

To download a copy of the insight report or full in-depth report, please visit **http://eti.co.uk/modelling-low-carbon-energy-system-designs-with-the-eti-esme-model**. To contact George Day, e-mail **george.day@eti.co.uk** or call him on 01509 202020.

The Energy Technologies Institute (ETI) brings together engineering projects that accelerate the development of affordable, secure and sustainable technologies that help the UK address its long-term emissions reductions targets as well as delivering nearer-term benefits. It is a public-private partnership between global energy and engineering companies – BP, Caterpillar, EDF, E.ON, Rolls-Royce and Shell – and the UK Government. Public sector representation is through the Department for Business, Innovation and Skills, with funding channelled through the Technology Strategy Board and the Engineering and Physical Sciences Research Council. The Department of Energy and Climate Change are observers on the Board. Further details: **http://eti.co.uk.**

Intellectual property for clean tech

Nick Sutcliffe at Mewburn Ellis discusses how to use the IP system to capture the full value of innovation in clean technology.

Innovation is a universal theme throughout all clean technologies. From nuclear fusion to fuel cells, the development of new or alternative technologies to reduce the environmental impact of human activity sets technical challenges that require innovative solutions.

Whilst some innovative solutions in clean technologies may represent major breakthroughs, others may be more mundane modifications or incremental improvements in existing technology or may involve the application of old technology in a new context. In all cases, however, innovation distinguishes a product or service from its competitors and plays a key role in its commercial success.

Innovative solutions do not come cheap. Bringing an innovative solution to market involves a significant investment of time and resources. Capturing the full market value of this investment is vital for businesses competing in intensively competitive global markets.

Intellectual property protects innovation

Imitators selling copy-cat products are a serious problem for innovators marketing clean tech products. Whilst the imitator benefits from the investment and ingenuity of the innovator for free, at the same time he reduces the potential rewards available to the innovator by competing in the market. Innovators can, however, protect themselves from imitators and reap the full rewards for their innovation using intellectual property (IP) rights. IP rights come in several different forms and different IP rights can be used to protect different aspects of a product from imitators.

Some IP rights, such as copyright, come into existence automatically. This type of right is very cheap to acquire and indeed, a business may be unaware of all the automatic IP rights that it actually possesses. Other IP rights, including patents, registered trademarks and registered designs, need to be actively sought and the application process may be tortuous and expensive. The acquisition of these rights therefore requires both a conscious decision by a business and a continuing level of commitment.

Although less grandiose than other IP rights, the trade secrets and know-how that a business necessarily acquires during is operations may be invaluable in differentiating it from its competitors. Even in the absence of other IP rights, the experience of actively developing a clean tech product is likely to give a business an edge over less-experienced competitors.

For any business operating in a clean technology field, an IP strategy that distinguishes a business and its products from the competition is likely to involve a combination of all these different forms of IP.

Intellectual property is a business asset

Intellectual property is usually associated with an offensive role; actively using your intellectual property to exclude competitors, preserving a market exclusively for you or those authorized by you to exploit. However, intellectual property rights also have other roles within the overall commercial strategy of a business.

Intellectual property rights may in themselves be used to generate revenue, either through licensing or selling. Intellectual property rights, and more generally a good intellectual property strategy, may also play a key role in attracting investors. Whilst investors are generally attracted to good science rather than good patents, the absence of an appropriate strategy for protecting the good science can often be a deal-breaker.

An intellectual property portfolio can also have a defensive role to play. It can deter competitors from enforcing their rights against you (for fear of retaliation) and any dispute might be settled by way of a cross-licence.

Of course, the same intellectual property rights may fulfil more than one of these roles. For example, a business may licence intellectual property rights for a country in which they do not themselves intend to operate, whilst retaining exclusive rights for countries in which they intend to do business. Similarly, non-core applications of a technology may be licensed out, while core applications are retained as the sole preserve of the business. This allows the business to extract the maximum value from its intellectual property.

On a wider level, by deterring the development of copycat products, intellectual property rights have the effect of encouraging competing businesses to develop their own technologies rather than copy each other. This drives innovation within the technical field as a whole.

Patents protect technical innovations

Patents are the key IP right for the protection of technical innovations. A technical innovation protected by a patent may be embodied in a commercial product and/or the processes for manufacturing or using a product.

Because it protects the underlying technical innovation, the patent protects more than just the commercial product or process, and is infringed by any competing product that employs the same underlying technical innovation, irrespective of whether or not the products look alike or not.

As products in clean technologies rely heavily on technical innovations to distinguish themselves from competitors, patents are likely to play an important role in the IP strategy of any business operating in this area.

Any technical innovation may be patentable

A technical innovation must meet certain legal criteria in order to qualify for patent protection. In particular, the innovation must be new and cannot be merely an obvious development of what is already known. Applications for patents undergo a rigorous examination process at Patent Offices around the world to ensure that patents are only granted for innovations that meet these criteria. Although this examination process is often slow, fast-track procedures are available for applications relating to green or clean technologies in some countries, including the UK and the United States.

Patents may be issued for innovations in any technical field from nuclear fusion to biofuels and may relate to any aspect of a product or process. For example, as well as a product as a whole a patent may cover a specific hardware or software component of a product or it may cover the use of a product in a particular application or process.

A patentable innovation may be an incremental improvement on a known product or a major breakthrough that opens up a whole new field or something in-between. The technical field of the innovation and its significance to the overall technical field is not important: as long as it fulfils the appropriate legal criteria, it qualifies for patent protection.

Strategies for intellectual property

Protecting an innovation with a patent is expensive and without clear focus, expenditure on patents can rapidly spiral out of control. Whether or not to pursue patent protection for a particular innovation will therefore depend on a judgement call of whether the innovation is important enough to the business plans of the business to justify the expenditure.

This decision may rest on the fundamental consideration of whether or not a business needs to be able to stop a competitor from replicating or copying the innovation, if it is to maintain its competitive advantage. Current or future revenue streams need to be considered. There is little point in focusing efforts on a product or service that is only ever going to find a small market, no matter how unique or innovative it may be, if in doing so there is no budget left for seeking protection for a less 'exciting' product or service that nevertheless accounts for a business's main stream of income.

A sound intellectual property strategy focuses on key assets and avoids unnecessary expenditure on protecting products and services that are less critical to the success of the business. It is also important to marry patent protection up with potential revenue streams. Sometimes it will pay off to focus protection more specifically on one or two particular revenue streams, rather than seeking very broad protection that may be harder and more expensive to obtain with little or no added benefit.

Management of intellectual property

The process of deciding whether or not to seek protection for a particular innovation requires serious consideration of a range of commercial issues.

However, once the decision to seek protection has been made, it is important that the innovator does not switch to an automatic default mode. It is all too easy to continue to drift along the same path, even when the commercial issues may have changed, and it may no longer be appropriate.

Continual active management is essential in order to get the best value from an IP portfolio. This means stopping at every decision point and taking stock of the overall business strategy and where this particular IP right fits in. Is an application appropriate? Can you drop it? Or do you need to take more protection?

Always take the time to evaluate whether the protection you are paying for still makes commercial sense. IP which does not add value to a business is simply a drain on resources which could be better used elsewhere.

Other people's intellectual property

In all of this, it must not be forgotten that competitors may well have their own IP rights. It is important to be aware of the impact that rights of others could have: at worst, these rights could halt the activities of a business completely. Rather than simply hoping for the best, prudent businesses will have in place strategies for dealing with third-party IP rights long before any problems become critical.

These strategies might include watching the IP filing activity of known competitors. This may allow a business to work around competitor's patents or other rights and/or to consider whether they might be vulnerable to attack. Watching a competitor's IP filing activity can also provide useful intelligence for their development work.

A wise business might also consider the arguably counter-intuitive possibility of publishing details of developments that they do not intend to protect themselves but that they intend to commercialize now or in the future. Such publication can prevent a competitor from later securing their own protection that might otherwise foreclose your ability to commercialize your own development.

And sometimes the best defence can be possession of your own portfolio of intellectual property rights.

Recycling old intellectual property

The old adage, 'there is nothing new under the sun' is particularly appropriate in the development of clean tech products. Old ideas from other technical fields may often be useful in solving new problems in clean technologies.

The patent literature is a vast and freely available resource that may be easily searched to find these old ideas. As long as the patents are no longer in force, the ideas described in them can be freely used by anybody. Furthermore, the adaptation of an old idea for use in a new clean technology application may itself give rise to new IP.

Innovation lies at the heart of the drive towards clean technologies and will be a cornerstone of successful businesses in this field. For these businesses, the development of an effective IP strategy will be invaluable in realizing the full value of this innovation and distinguishing themselves from their competitors in the global market.

Nick Sutcliffe is a partner in Mewburn Ellis LLP, one of Europe's premier IP firms, with over 60 patent and trademark attorneys and technical specialists, covering the full range of intellectual property issues: patents (in all technology areas), trade marks, designs, industrial copyright and related matters.

Nick Sutcliffe has a BSc in Biochemistry from University of Bristol and a PhD in Biochemistry from University of Leicester. Nick spent four years working in industrial research and development before joining Mewburn Ellis in 1997. He qualified as a Chartered Patent Attorney and European Patent Attorney in 2001 and became a partner at Mewburn Ellis in 2003. Nick's work is mainly in the biotechnology field.

Further information is available from Mewburn Ellis LLP, 33 Gutter Lane, London EC2V 8AS (tel: 020 7776 5300; e-mail: **nick.sutcliffe@mewburn.com**; website: **www.mewburn.com**).

PART FOUR
Re-thinking energy

New demands on electricity

Mark Thompson and **Martin Queen** at the Energy Innovation Centre review the potential for innovation in the UK's electricity networks.

The UK electricity networks have evolved since the latter 19th century from simple direct current systems, which carried power from municipal power stations to street lights and privileged citizens' houses, to a ubiquitous necessity in modern life. However, the evolution of these networks has started to change in recent years from power generated centrally and fed out radially, to one where electricity generation can appear at almost any point in the network with the advent of distributed electricity generation from wind farms, combined heat and power plants, photovoltaic generators and more. To add further challenges and complexity, the energy we use per head or per pound of GDP has risen dramatically over the years and is set to increase further with the electrification of heat and transport.

It's important to note that much of the infrastructure is over 60 years old; built in the days when all railway locomotives were powered by steam and the automobile industry was still building motor-cars with chassis and wooden frames! So it's a whole new world for a whole lot of old copper.

To add even more pressure, customers expect electricity supply to be available at all times with no interruptions, whereas at one time electricity was a luxury. This combined set of challenges has led to regulatory and political pressure on networks to innovate. There is therefore a significant opportunity for innovation to create new services and products within electrical networks due to the above pressures and trends.

This article seeks to explore the technological challenges created by the changing public and political attitudes and issues posed by a new generation mix and use profile whilst highlighting the opportunities for innovation to address these challenges.

In simple terms, the challenge for our energy system as a whole is one of meeting electricity demand 'wherever it might be, at whatever magnitude' with supply 'from wherever it comes from' on a minute-by-minute, season-by-season and year-by-year basis, using an electricity distribution network that was designed for a completely different way of working.

Needs for cost reduction and improvements in efficiency across such a large national system automatically create commercial opportunities to meet those needs. The UK energy system can be broken down into three portions: 1) energy generation; 2) energy use and, sitting in the middle; 3) energy distribution; each with its own opportunities for innovation.

Innovation in energy generation

Our mix of energy sources comprises a very diverse spectrum each with its own particular characteristics. Table 4.1.1 below illustrates some of these, and the spectrum of alignments with some of our energy sources.

TABLE 4.1.1   Characteristics and spectrum of a range of energy sources

Energy source characteristic	The spectrum	
Magnitude/scale	Large – Nuclear, gas, coal	Small – Microgeneration eg solar
Carbon impact	Poor – Coal/gas	Good – hydroelectric, nuclear, wind
Response time to ramp up/down	Slow – Nuclear, coal	Fast – hydroelectric, wind
Predictability	Easy to predict – Gas/coal/nuclear/tidal	Hard to predict – wind/tidal/solar
Cost/unit energy	Low – coal/gas	High – offshore wind, wave/tidal
ROI timescales	Quick payback – solar	Slow payback – nuclear

So why is there need for innovation in any of the above?

With the increasing cost of energy and increasingly spiky and unpredictable energy usage, the UK ideally needs an energy source that is: low cost + high capacity + low carbon + is predictable + has very quick response times.

Unfortunately, no such energy source currently exists, at least not in the UK, so combining and managing the above mix is the imperative we have to work with. The innovation opportunities for energy generation are therefore for technologies or commercial approaches that can modify or improve any of the above; the aim being to develop technologies to work collectively, more efficiently and as a diversified portfolio of energy sources, ie to:

- make less responsive energy sources more responsive;
- improve predictability of less predictable sources;
- reduce the carbon impact of poorly performing sources;
- reduce the investment requirement or speed up the deployment of sources with poor ROI timescales.

Innovation in energy use

Taking the domestic scenario alone, in a traditional domestic dwelling in the UK the actual electrical load is very low on average, although it has generally been on an upward trend over the decades. Steady growth such as this is not such an issue in itself as it can be planned for and coping measures put in place. There has also been a growth in many other significant electrical loads that cumulatively add to the challenge. There are familiar loads such as the growth in high power electric showers, induction cooker hobs and tumble-dryers.

But there are fresh new challenges also. As discussed earlier there are more unpredictable energy sources appearing on the network, however there are also significant *new* energy loads that will start to become much more common on the customer demand side, namely electric vehicles and low-carbon electrification of domestic heating with heat pumps. The energy consumption of these technologies are of a similar magnitude to the energy demand of say, a domestic electric oven or kettle, except of course they are likely to be powered for much longer periods. They are also not terribly predictable as to exactly how and when they will be installed or powered. The 'match-supply-to-demand' maths just got harder!

The most challenging is electric vehicles which have the potential to be turned on anywhere at any time! With the increase in electric vehicle and heat pump uptake there is the potential for large loads to be connected simultaneously. Think of the worst-case situation, of people coming home from work and plugging in their EV cars to charge then putting the heat pump heating on, putting the kettle on for a cup of tea and then starting to cook a meal. Changes in work patterns compared to historic norms also add to uncertainty in energy use forecasting. This overall recipe leads to less predictable timing of demand, with higher peak demands than the network was designed for. The effects of these two factors in simple terms are as follows:

Higher peaks = hotter assets in the distribution network = reduced life and increased failures = increased maintenance costs + risks to network reliability.

PLUS, unforeseen peaks = sources of generation are unable to match supply to demand = rapid and usually carbon intensive or costly generation ramp up or down = additional costs/energy unit + risk to quality or reliability to supply.

The traditional alternative to the above is to upgrade the power handling capacity of the existing electricity network = heavier copper + bigger distribution assets + bigger distribution towers (pylons) + more generation = significant expense and disruption for many years + energy users absorbing the costs of the expensive energy source solutions.

So, in response to the above the smart approach for the domestic scenario is to seek out innovation opportunities and value propositions in the following areas:

- reducing the energy used in buildings per se;
- improved building fabric (thereby indirectly reducing heating demand);
- improved knowledge of impending load or improved forecasting;
- shifting loads away from peak times, either through commercial incentive mechanisms, technology or encouraging different energy user behaviours (or a combination of all three).

This last area, one of energy user behaviours is perhaps the most challenging of all. Overcoming energy user habits, the lack of understanding of energy, attitudes towards energy and creating value propositions that overcome these characteristics will require the most creativity in technical, commercial, social and psychological innovation. Energy users are ultimately huge components of this 'whole system' so if we can involve them as part of the solution then the outcomes will be far more successful.

Innovation in electricity distribution

So with energy generation on one side of the equation and energy users on the other, the gateway between them is our distribution network that has to cope with all of the new supply/demand uncertainties and to stay reliable in a world that is very different to the one it was designed for.

Figure 4.1.1 shows the various areas that generation can be present in a network overlaid to the traditional top-down energy distribution approach.

In the past large centrally located power plants had a uni-directional flow of power down through the networks to customers. Energy sources can now come from potentially anywhere on the system and yet as we have discussed above, the two sides, energy generation and energy use are becoming less predictable, with higher peaks, and which also implies bigger differentials between peaks and troughs.

You may well ask why this is a problem for the networks as you would think copper and aluminium are pretty robust materials when used as electrical conductors. One of the most important reasons, alluded to earlier, is that of heat, and heat stress. When electricity flows, the conductors it travels through give off heat.

The effects of this are:

Large power flows = large quantities of heat = more rapid asset degradation (eg materials such as insulators) = reduced asset life = unpredictable failures + increased asset maintenance + reduced lifetime.

PLUS, rapid rise or fall in the match between supply and demand = rapid rises or falls in the above heat = rapid thermal expansion/contraction of hardware = lower life and reliability issues.

FIGURE 4.1.1   Electrical distribution network

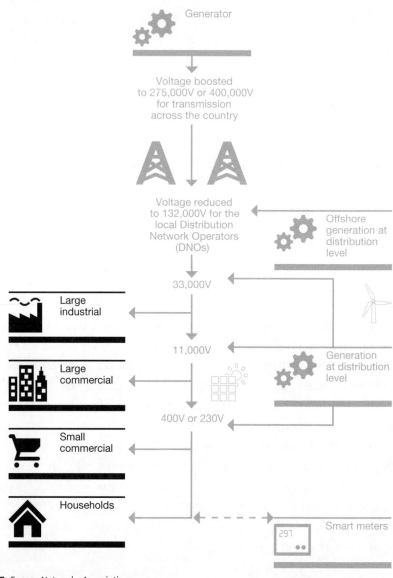

SOURCE: Energy Networks Association
http://goo.gl/cc39zO

Demand and supply imbalances are therefore keenly felt in the electricity networks in the form of reliability and operational costs of the network and so represent a commercial opportunity for innovations to improve these scenarios.

So, the opportunities for innovation in the electricity distribution networks are:

- low-cost solutions to monitor the thermal stress and power conditions being experienced in potentially any part of the network;

- increased visibility and pre-emptive knowledge of demand/supply imbalances so that mitigation action can be taken;

- low-cost, high-capacity, space-efficient energy storage technology – if you can store or bank bulk electricity efficiently in some manner then you can use that banked energy as a buffer to smooth out the peaks and troughs;

- smart/autonomous systems for enabling electricity grids to dynamically self-reconfigure in response to changing circumstances or in response to faults;

- innovations or systems to influence or control energy users at times of critical network stress to reduce peaks, sudden changes and smooth the demand profile;

- thermal modelling, asset condition monitoring, predictive maintenance innovations, failure prediction tools;

- innovations that enable existing hardware or new hardware and materials to run hotter.

Conclusion

So, it is a challenging world for the UK electricity network. Power could come from anywhere, heavy loads (particularly electric vehicles) can appear anywhere and adapting to it has to be done invisibly, cheaply, dynamically and seamlessly in a world where the customer has greater dependency and expectations than ever before.

This must surely then be one of the most exciting times to be involved with our energy system, comparing only with the time of the original national grid network rollout 50-plus years ago. The key differences between then and now though, is that the challenge is not just a technical one, but also one of finding value propositions for all parties including, most importantly, propositions that win the hearts and minds and engagement of energy users.

The jigsaw puzzle is big and complex, and only by innovation and creativity will we meet the challenge.

Mark Thompson heads up the innovation project team at the Energy Innovation Centre. His background and experience encompass engineering, manufacturing, project management, technology development and commercialization, and marketing.

Martin Queen is the lead electrical engineer at the Energy Innovation Centre with responsibility for electrical innovations. Martin's experience includes working in the power distribution sector in both a utility and consultancy environment.

The Energy Innovation Centre is a not for profit SME that partners with the energy network companies in Great Britain. Its role is to discover, develop and deploy innovations that enable the energy networks to reduce cost, improve flexibility and facilitate the migration to a low carbon energy system. It specializes in seeking innovations from small to medium enterprises and from sources outside the conventional supply chain and outside the UK.

For further information and to see lists of specific innovation opportunities see **www.energyinnovationcentre.com**.

Smart energy

For winners in clean tech, look at those who manage data best, suggests **Andrew Mitchell** at the CleanWeb Factory.

When you hear the phrase 'Green ICT' you are likely to think about your IT department reminding you to switch off your PC before you go home or perhaps something more sophisticated such as a server room being replaced by moving systems to the 'cloud'. Granted the ICT industry has a big (and growing) carbon footprint, weighing in at around 2–4 per cent of total global emissions, equivalent to the airline industry. However, 'data science, informatics and computer science' have a much larger role to play in reducing the other 96 per cent of global emissions. For example, there are potential low-carbon and energy aspects in each of the Scottish Informatics and Computer Science Alliance (**www.sicsa.ac.uk**) research themes of:

- next generation internet;
- complex systems engineering;
- human-computer interaction;
- modelling and abstraction;
- future cities.

Here I would like to explore smart meters and smart grids as two key aspects of the ICT-enabled transition to a low-carbon economy. Most households in the UK will have a smart meter by 2020; the government is requiring, rather than enforcing, energy suppliers to make this so. This has the *potential* to make a significant impact on the way we consume energy. Sources of energy supply are diversifying in the forms of district heat networks, biomass, wind, wave and tidal. The proliferation of electric vehicles changes the geography and timing of our energy demand too. These changing sources and consumption patterns require a significant upgrade to the national grid – specifically to grids we can sense, measure and collect data from, ie smart grids.

Typically when people talk about smart meters and smart grids their emphasis is on technology and infrastructure; and on critical issues such as privacy, security and industry standards. What I would like to explore here is: the global context, the energy efficiency business opportunity, consumer behaviour and *super-useful information*: Who will win?

The global context

Climate change is serious business. In his recent blog,[1] Sir Richard Branson urged businesses to stand up to climate change deniers; Bill Gates is investing in next-generation nuclear and carbon capture and storage ventures.[2] Even the language of hardcore climate scientists is changing to recognize that the 'fix' needs to be market driven: 'We live in an era of man-made climate change... Investments in better preparation can pay dividends both for the present and for the future.' (Vicente Barros, Meteorologist, Intergovernmental Panel on Climate Change, Yokohama, Japan, 31 March 2014).

We have to be honest here and recognize that this global challenge is not going to be fixed by 'Tom and Barbara' cutting their household emissions by 20 per cent following the rollout of smart meters in Surbiton. Our efficiency savings will be dwarfed by the new energy required to bring clean water to an estimated 3.4 billion people, and electricity to 1.2 billion people currently in the dark, predominantly in Africa and India. The global challenge also sits with China's energy consumption rising 148 per cent from 1990 to 2008 (according to data from the International Energy Agency). Immense growth in the 'BRIC' economies, fuelled by dirty coal, oil and gas.

Despite this bewildering global challenge, there is a decent contribution to be made through smart infrastructure and living the 'good life'. Not least because those of us from countries who started this journey of industrialization back in the 18th century have a global obligation and duty to do so.

Consumer behaviour

Let's assume every house has a smart meter and with miraculous acceleration of government policy and investment we have smart grids rolled out across the UK. The infrastructure is there, the technology is easy – job done.

Not so, in my opinion. In the UK we waste a horrific amount of food, water, heat and electricity – and we are not motivated financially or otherwise to change. Of course I am not disregarding fuel and food poverty in the UK and the challenges that many face. But this is relative poverty to those afore-mentioned 3.4 billion people who do not have access to clean drinking water.

Maybe it is time to admit defeat and embrace this concept of us being too rich and too lazy to change. Instead, let us flip it round to ask if we can use information and communication technologies to make life and this transition to a low-carbon economy easier. If money is not a motivator for reducing consumption we can do at least two things: one, let computer systems and automation take over within parameters we set; and two, find new motivations. An obvious motivation is peer pressure. How much energy do I consume compared to my neighbours or work colleagues? The 'gamifi-cation of energy' is upon us, with some companies recognizing the potential of peer pressure. I am sure that Facebook will have a dominant role to play in this space too.

Super-useful information: who will win?

It is slightly paradoxical that energy utility companies are the ones who are being tasked and pressured by the government to deliver smart and efficient energy. It's much like the drinks industry doing a U-turn and backing a minimum price-per-unit of alcohol – or turkeys voting for Christmas. Utility companies are being asked to sell less to their customers. I think the winners in this space are going to be media and communications companies like BSkyB, BT, Virgin Media, the aforementioned Facebook or perhaps an aggregator such as Marks & Spencer or Tesco.

Why? Well the fact is that 'smart meters' and 'smart grids' are actually very dumb. Data on their own are useless. We need insight and wisdom to enable action. Wisdom is one of those concepts with many complex definitions, but it has been neatly and simply described as 'super useful information'.

BSkyB, BT, Virgin and Tesco already know more about your behaviour than you do. We happily, perhaps unwittingly, allow Facebook to take this level of insight to a creepy extreme. My energy utility company knows absolutely nothing about me and very little about my surroundings. So in comparison, they are massively disadvantaged in understanding consumer behaviour. There is a widely adopted 'wisdom hierarchy' that has a pyramid with 'data' at the base, followed by 'information' and 'knowledge' and then 'wisdom' at the top. This to me encapsulates perfectly the technical and commercial gap we have with the smart meter and smart grid agenda. At the moment we are predominantly operating at the base of the triangle, being driven by energy utility companies that have bigger problems to deal with (global energy prices, increasing competition of supply, hefty fines for misleading customers and so on). The journey from the physical hardware, data and network layers of smart energy infrastructure up through all the communication layers to an application (eg a web browser or smart phone app) and then finally to the all-important human-computer interaction piece, requires some serious innovation. Serious and radical innovation does not flow abundantly through the blood of energy utility companies, at least not since the days of Nikola Tesla and Newcastle-upon-Tyne's Charles Merz.

ICT, media and retail companies are key to delivering this smart future. Therefore it's critical to see more collaboration between these companies, energy utility companies and applied academics from the fields of Informatics and Computer Science and Arts, Humanities and Social Science; to work on this challenge of *super-useful information* and consumer behaviour.

Andrew Mitchell is Managing Director of CleanWeb Factory Ltd, a company that delivers executive education and innovation programmes for high-growth ventures, corporates and public sector leaders. Andrew is a programme manager with 19 years' experience in the ICT sector and 12 years' experience in business-university collaboration and commercialization. He has worked for small businesses, FTSE100 corporations and world leading research-intensive universities; internationally in Scotland, England, Spain, North America, Australia, China and India. From 2011 to 2013, he was a Business Manager at the Edinburgh Centre for Carbon Innovation, a 30 million-euro 'low carbon innovation hub'. Prior to this he established and grew Informatics Ventures, based in Europe's largest and Britain's highest-quality Computer Science department.

Further information is available from Andrew Mitchell (tel: 07793 111386; e-mail: **andrew.mitchell@cleanwebfactory.com;** Twitter: **http://twitter.com/roomitchell**; website: **www.cleanwebfactory.com**).

Notes

1 http://www.virgin.com/richard-branson/businesses-should-stand-up-to-climate-change-deniers [acessed 6 May 2014].

2 http://hbr.org/product/TerraPower/an/813108-PDF-ENG [acessed 6 May 2014].

The supergrid

The world has plenty of cheap renewable power, says **Godfrey Spickernell** of Atlantic Supergrid, but can we connect it up?

Perhaps the most remarkable supergrid enthusiast was American inventor Richard Buckminster Fuller, born in 1895. He believed that electricity was a powerful force for development and civilization, and proposed 'the interconnection of electric power networks between regions and continents into a global energy grid, with an emphasis on tapping abundant renewable energy resources – a world wide web of electricity'. This map shows the extent of his extraordinary vision:

FIGURE 4.3.1   Richard Buckminster Fuller's vision of a future Supergrid

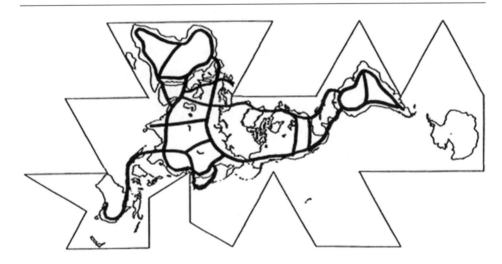

We now have the potential to realize a limited version of these ideas. The prize could indeed be abundant, clean, low-cost energy.

Harnessing the power of the planet

Solar radiation arriving on Earth is equivalent to something like 6,000 times our current human energy requirements. Much of this energy is needed to power our planet's wind, hydrological and photosynthesis systems, but there is still plenty for mankind to harvest.

The only problem is the best renewable resources tend to be in remote places such as the polar wastes, the mountains, deserts, volcanoes and the middle of the ocean. If we could collect a small fraction and transport it efficiently to our homes, we could have more cheap power than we know what do with. For example, the 'world square' on Figure 4.3.2 shows Desertec's assessment of the area of the Sahara that would need to be covered with solar thermal generators to provide the world's electricity. The same concept applies to other remote sources of energy, such as wind from the northern seas.

A European energy supergrid

Dr Gregor Czisch of Kassel University is credited with developing the original European supergrid concept. He considered whether it would be possible to meet all of Europe's power needs with renewable electricity at reasonable cost, using a wide-area supergrid, extending from Iceland to the Sahara and out as far as Arabia and Kazakhstan.

To answer the question, he first identified the available energy resources – wind, solar, hydro, biomass, etc – and analysed their locations, production characteristics and seasonality to ensure there was sufficient supply at all times. He then considered hydro-energy storage facilities in mountainous regions such as Scandinavia and Switzerland. Finally he identified the key European demand centres. Then it was simply a matter of plugging the data into a computer and programming it to work out the optimal grid connections to link the system together. The result was as shown in Figure 4.3.3 on page 126.

FIGURE 4.3.2 Desertec's assessment of the area of the Sahara that would need to be covered with solar thermal generators to provide the world's electricity

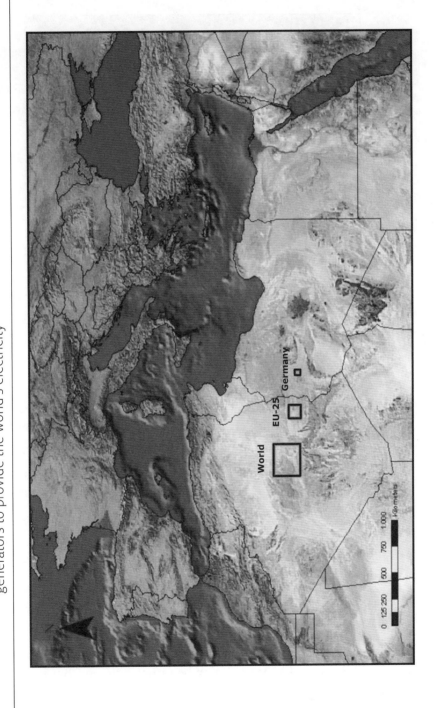

FIGURE 4.3.3   Dr Gregor Czisch's European supergrid concept

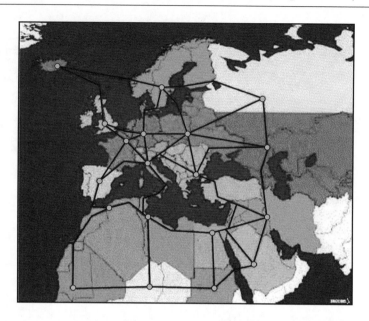

Dr Czisch's conclusions were:

- A wind-based system was the most practical because:

  (a) onshore wind is relatively low cost and;

  (b) it is generally windy in the north in winter, and in the south in summer. It would require limited biomass back up during continent-wide low-wind periods.

- Such a system, he estimated, could deliver power at 0.047 euro per kilowatt-hour (kWh) – the UK wholesale price is some £0.04 per kilowatt-hour today.

- 750 gigawatts (GW) of extra transmission capacity would be required.

- Existing hydro capacity is sufficient to meet European demand for six weeks.

It should be noted that this is one theoretical study, and the realities and costs of building a real supergrid may be rather different. But it is an inspiring thought, nonetheless.

The energy grids we have today

Before thinking about a supergrid, what of our existing AC electricity grids? The 2011 BBC documentary, *The Secret Life of the National Grid* is an excellent introduction to this hidden world, celebrating the epic achievement of grid construction and explaining how it has, quite simply, enabled the modern world. The advent of reliable electricity has changed our lives radically, and brought about the present hyper-connected age of internet technology.

Grids help to make electricity cheap and reliable. Without a grid, individual stations can only power a local area, and when the station is down, the power is off. They also help us to tackle the most frustrating question at the heart of electricity supply – balancing supply with demand. Engineers would prefer us to use the same amount of electricity all day long; it would then be a simple matter of devising a cheap and efficient system to provide it. However, in the real world peaks and troughs occur over the 24-hour cycle, and at other times. For example, UK demand can fluctuate between 20 gigawatts on a summer night to more than 60 gigawatts on a cold winter's evening. As electricity is hard to store, supply must be constantly matched with demand. We also need spare capacity idling in the background (so-called 'spinning reserve') in case a station goes offline, or demand surges unexpectedly. A country-wide grid allows us to coordinate an electricity system that matches these requirements efficiently, provides reserve capacity and brings power to the remotest houses, all at an affordable price.

Why fluctuating demand increases costs

Continuous demand can be met with 'base-load' plant working 24/7. These plants, typically coal- or nuclear-powered, tend to be large, with low running costs but a high capital cost. The high capital cost is no problem if it can be amortized over a large and constant long-term volume of electricity sales via the grid; the result is cheap power. Variable-demand segments are catered for by switching more flexible generators on or off as required. Typically there is a hierarchy of plants with increasingly higher running cost/lower capital cost, which are brought online as needed. Final minute-by-minute balancing can be provided by hydro plants or spinning reserve. This cost hierarchy means the average price of electricity is higher than it would be if using base-load alone.

How grids make electricity cheaper

The larger your grid-networked area, the greater the potential for supplying a higher proportion of cheap base-load power. In theory, Buckminster Fuller's vision could provide a similar mechanism on a wider scale. Imagine Europe and the United States connected by a giant high-capacity grid network. Given the time differences, you could share the generation capacity, and shut down much of the high cost plant in both Europe and the United States. And why stop at the United States? The wider the area you cover, the greater the benefit. Eventually it would make sense for the whole world to be connected, just as Buckminster Fuller envisaged.

Renewables are changing the shape of the grid

Grids were designed to bring power from a few large centralized power stations and feed it to centres of demand. Those stations were located near supplies of fuel (generally gas or coal) and access to cooling water. Nuclear stations were located around the coast, in relatively remote places. As we diversify the power sector and commission more renewables, we will have to re-orientate our grids. Already some output from wind farms has to be spilled, both in the UK and Germany, when the grid is overloaded. Having committed to taking its nuclear stations off line, Germany will have to install some 10 gigawatts of new north-south transmission capacity, as its surplus wind generation is far from the demand centres in the south.

The emergence of a supergrid

Unbeknown to most of us, the world already has a surprising amount of interconnection and long-distance transmission. The age of the supergrid is dawning, but organically, and without a master plan. Take a look at Northern Europe, for example – in Figure 4.3.4, the darker lines represent existing connectors, and the lighter planned ones.

There are plenty of interconnectors in other parts of the world too (called 'interties' in the United States). Figure 4.3.5 gives an idea of the extent of the existing high-voltage, direct current (HVDC) links around the world (although it is not necessarily complete).

FIGURE 4.3.4 Northern Europe – planned and existing connectors

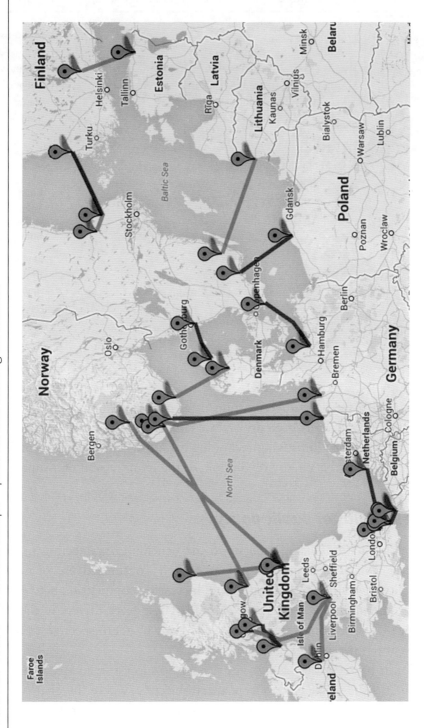

FIGURE 4.3.5   High Voltage Direct Current HVDC links around the world

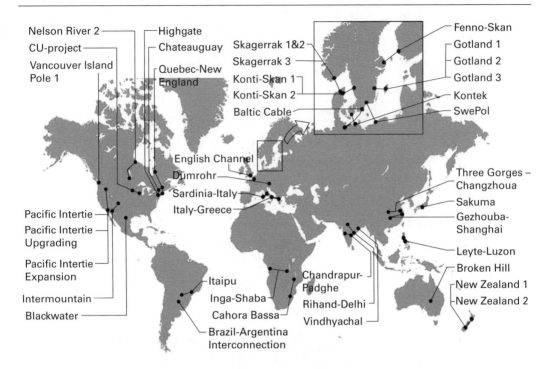

The trend towards interconnection of electricity systems goes back to the 1960s, and has largely been driven by a combination of economics and public policy (as well as improving technological know-how) and had little to do with the renewable energy revolution, or the grand vision of a supergrid.

The stimulus of public policy

Individual nations have understood the benefits of connecting to a neighbouring country's electricity system, such as: optimized use of generation capacity, diversification of supply and increasing competition between generators, potentially lowering costs overall. These were drivers in the original France-UK interconnection, which was built by the respective state-owned grid entities for mutual national benefit.

For its part, the EU has two key reasons to support increased connectivity: the first is the single electricity market objective, where the goal is to move towards harmonizing electricity prices across the entire European region; and the second is to help meet the goal of 80 per cent renewable energy by 2050.

The economic drivers for an interconnector

Besides public policy, there are commercial reasons for developers to build interconnectors:

1 Savings can be made where two regions have different times for peak demand (the greater the difference the better). An interconnector will allow them to share the output of lower-cost plant and divert the output as required, enabling the operator to profit from an arbitrage trade.

2 Those with a cheap, underutilized resource may want to gain access to market. Examples include the Pacific DC Intertie, which brings power from the Columbia River Dams to California, and projects in Canada, Brazil and, more recently, the Three Gorges Dam in China, which supplies power to Shanghai 600 miles away. The new proposed link between the UK and Norway seeks to exploit Norway's capacity to deliver hydro-power on demand and may provide a means to store some of the UK's surplus wind output.

3 The requirement for renewables is beginning to play its part. Harnessing the UK's resources requires a massive reorganization of the present UK grid. Investments are already under way, mainly by new commercial entrants into the offshore transmission market to connect the new wind farms. These connections may even end up connecting to another country's offshore grid, hence establishing de facto interconnectors.

Improvements in technology

Over the last century, the HVDC technologies involved in long-distance transmission have steadily improved. It is now possible to transmit power with losses as low as 3 per cent per 1,000 kilometres. Transmission voltages have increased, AC-DC conversion has become more efficient, and new modes of DC operation such as voltage source commutation have been important in connecting projects without a stable grid on each end, such as offshore wind. Technical progress continues with the additional promise of efficient DC circuit breaking. (See technical section on AC v DC systems below.)

There have been efforts on the AC front as well. Europe has begun unifying the continental grids so there is now one synchronous zone across most of the EU, and there are further ambitions to unify the European and Russian grids. However, the larger the area in a synchronous AC zone, the more problems can arise such as looping – where energy takes an unexpected path across the network – congestion, and rogue electricity flows.

The most likely path of emergence

Just as with the internet, the supergrid will most likely emerge from the activities of many people in different places at different times, gradually linking together to form a network. Each component will be a valuable and worthwhile enterprise in its own right, selecting the most promising stranded resources, developing them, and building the required infrastructure to bring the power to market. The first steps have already been taken, with rapid deployment of HVDC wind-farm connections in the North Sea and increasing interconnection between countries.

What could the supergrid do for renewable energy?

In due course, renewables may become cost-competitive by steady improvement, or if for example fossil generators are forced to fully price in the cost of CO_2 emission, but this is unlikely to happen any time soon. Meanwhile, renewables face two key stumbling blocks: cost and intermittency. So how can grids help them through these barriers?

Help with the cost problem

Consider wind: the power available in wind depends on the cube of the wind speed. Therefore a site with 10 miles-per-hour average winds is not just twice as good as a site with 5 miles-per-hour winds, but eight times as good. Even better (all else being equal) the electricity can be an eighth of the cost. Similar laws apply to other types of renewable energy. So there is a huge premium on exploiting the best resources. But where are they? As we have seen above, they tend to be far from where we live. In Europe, they are around the periphery, where it is hottest and windiest – sun and wind from the African deserts, wind and wave from the northern seas, etc. The cube rule should give us hope for ultimately undercutting fossil fuels. Even now, using sub-optimal resources, today's solar and wind technologies are already moving towards grid parity. How much better would it be if we could bring the power from the regions with the best renewable resources? The supergrid could be the key breakthrough that will enable us to transition to a cheaper and better energy system.

Help with the intermittency problem

There are various ways to tackle intermittency:

1 Harvest wind from a wider geographical spread – it is always blowing somewhere. If your catchment area spreads across a continent and beyond, you have a better chance.

2 Coordinate the seasonal variation between resources to smooth things out – for example, it is helpful that peak wind in the Sahara region is in the summer, while in the north it occurs in winter.

3 Use a range of complementary technologies – for example wind, sun, hydro, biomass, geothermal, wave, etc.

4 Build sufficient redundancy into the system, so that when one source is not functioning sufficiently, it is replaced by others.

5 Hold dispatchable power such as hydro and biomass in reserve, so they can be used like a giant battery as and when required.

6 Use demand-response management technologies to time-shift and smooth electricity usage. For example, smart washing machines can be programmed to wait and only start up when they sense cheap electricity is available. Demand management is an aspect of what is referred to as the smart grid. It is a useful adjunct to the supergrid, and ultimately may lead to our grids becoming both super and smart – ie *supersmart*, as lobby group, 'Friends of the Supergrid' likes to refer to it.

However you decide to go about solving the intermittency and cost problems, a supergrid can be of great assistance.

Supergrid projects in development

In Europe alone there are several planned marine HVDC interconnections in the pipeline, as shown below. Figure 4.3.6 focuses on wind energy in particular, with existing links and others in various stages of planning or development. Figure 4.3.7 shows a wider perspective, and shows (in dotted lines) planned links to North Africa and the proposed UK-Iceland link, which would be the longest marine cable in the world.

There are also considerable improvements being made on land-based networks, and of course much activity in other parts of the world, including the United States and Canada, as the lists of projects by the various contractors such as ABB, Siemens, Alstom, Prysmian and Nexans and others will testify. China is rapidly expanding its HVDC cable network, and has begun to compete in developing the next generation of technology, led by the State Grid Corporation of China.

FIGURE 4.3.6   Wind energy links in various stages of planning and development

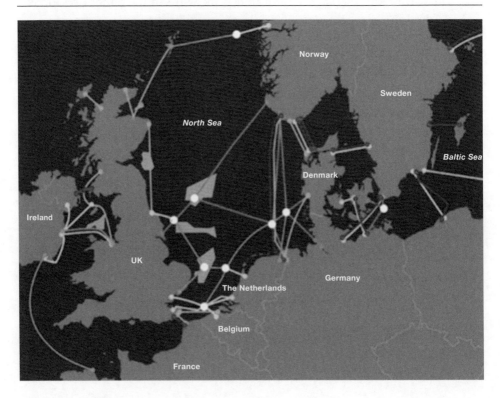

FIGURE 4.3.7 Energy links – a wider European perspective

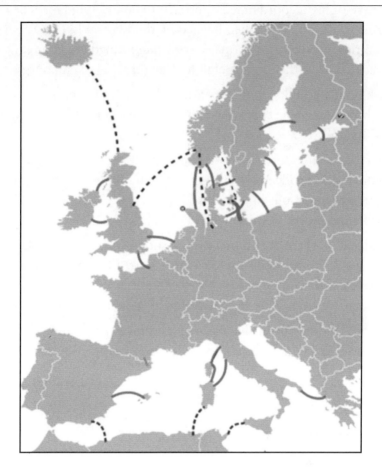

Supergrid supporters and proponents

The community of supergrid supporters is active and vociferous, and even includes politicians such as David Cameron. Supportive industry bodies, political, and other groupings include:

1 The EU itself, which actively promotes pan-European energy infrastructure, interconnections and connections with neighbouring regions. There are various established functions such as the European Network of Transmission System Operators for Electricity (ENTSO-E), and supportive instruments such as Projects of Common Interest and the Connecting Europe Facility, part of the European Infrastructure Package.

2 The North Sea Countries Offshore Grid Initiative has the objective of developing a coordinated approach to connecting North Sea wind farms in a rational manner. Backed by the EU and ENTSO-E, the countries involved are: Germany, the United Kingdom, France, Denmark, Sweden, the Netherlands, Belgium, Ireland and Luxembourg.

3 Irish-Scottish Links on Energy Study (ISLES) is a proposal to link offshore renewable energy generation in Scotland, Northern Ireland and Ireland.

4 Desertec is an industry consortium of predominantly German companies. The idea is to encourage the building of concentrating solar power stations in North Africa and the Middle East and export the power to Europe by HVDC lines.

5 Medgrid is a French-inspired project along similar lines to Desertec, which aims to promote and develop a Euro-Mediterranean electricity network that would provide North Africa and Europe with inexpensive renewable electricity, mostly solar.

6 Friends of the Supergrid is a non-government association that promotes the policy agenda for a European supergrid, and is led by grid-enthusiast Dr Eddie O'Connor.

Bolstering existing AC grids

Our existing grids are not designed to support the current level of renewables, let alone what is in the pipeline. It is clear that large investments are needed – but how do we arrange this is an optimal manner? Ideally it would be sensible to design links today in such a way that they will one day become the building blocks of a pan-European supergrid. The EU's E-Highway 2050 project is charged with the task of thinking ahead to create just such a plan.

Meanwhile the individual countries are hard at work. In the UK the imperative is to overcome the bottlenecks between Scotland, where much of the UK's renewable power is generated, and the rest of the country. The centrepiece is a plan for two new HVDC marine cables called the 'bootstraps': one on the west (2.2 gigawatts), and one on the east, at a later stage of development (see Figure 4.3.8).

FIGURE 4.3.8 Plans for moving power south from Scotland, including two new HVDC marine cables, one on each coast ('bootstraps')

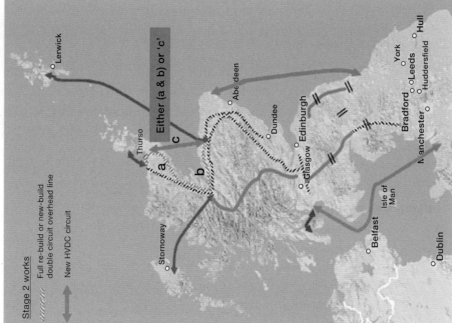

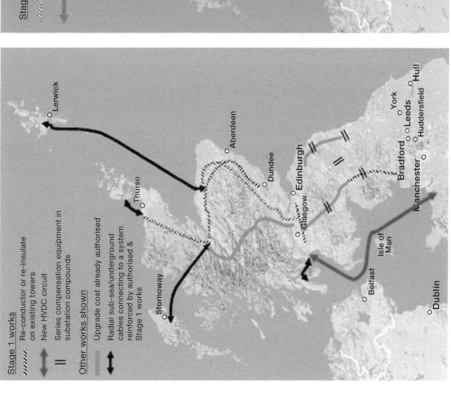

As mentioned, in Germany the issue is to move the 10 gigawatts or so of surplus wind power from the north down to the south. The plan is to run HVDC cables along the existing AC corridors where possible, so as to overcome objections to new transmission lines, at a projected cost of some 10 billion euros.

In the United States, plans are less well-advanced, but the renewable industry has made proposals for grid strengthening. This is the American Wind Energy Association's suggestion for a 765-kilovolt (kV) AC transmission grid designed to carry 400 gigawatts of wind power to cities from the Midwest at a cost of US $60 billion.

FIGURE 4.3.9   The American Wind Energy Association's proposed 765-kilovolt (kV) AC transmission grid

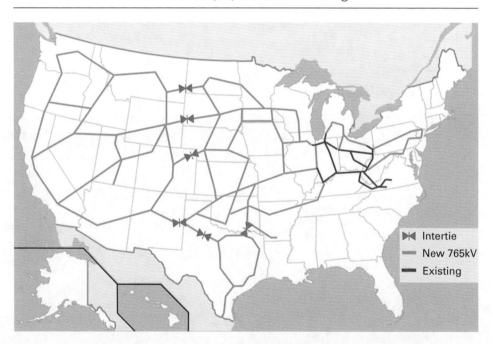

AC or DC? And the promise of a revolutionary breakthough in DC

At the beginning of the electrical age, Thomas Edison favoured a direct current (DC) grid, while George Westinghouse and Nikolai Tesla promoted alternating current (AC). In what became known as the 'battle of the currents',

AC eventually won. It turned out to be the natural choice, as it has several advantages, such as the ease of stepping voltages up and down (allowing us to transmit efficiently at high voltage but to step the power down for local distribution); the ease of breaking a circuit even at very high voltage and the ability to create a resilient network. This is why our existing grids are based on AC.

However, AC is not perfect. One drawback is that every time the current alternates, it wastes some energy creating subsidiary induced currents in the wire itself and in the surroundings, leading to greater transmission losses than for DC. Where the cable is surrounded by a relatively good conductor like water, the effect is more pronounced. After a certain distance under water, about 80 kilometres or so, an AC cable may not produce any net current, as the energy can be fully used up creating these capacitance/induction losses.

DC also has an edge in that it uses the whole core of the wire to carry the current, whereas AC prefers to travel through the circumference (the so-called 'skin effect'), which means DC wires can carry more current for a given wire, and can easily be made thicker to carry more, and DC does not suffer from dielectric or even coronal losses to the same extent.

Despite the advantage in more efficient transmission, the inability of DC to work like AC has held it back. One of the biggest problems is circuit breaking: you can switch large AC currents on and off because at one point in their cycle the current is zero. By contrast DC is always on, so to break the circuit you literally need to cut the wire somehow. That is OK with small currents, but with enough energy coming down a cable to power a small city, the result would be dangerous and explosive arcing.

Power engineers have been working on this problem for a long time, and at the time of writing they are becoming excited, as the potential Holy Grail of an efficient HVDC circuit breaker is in sight. Companies such as Alstom, ABB and Siemens each have their favoured solutions. If it works, it should be possible to build HVDC networks along similar lines to HVAC networks, massively widening the scope for integrated long distance transmission, reducing costs, and lowering losses, bringing a truly networked HVDC supergrid within reach.

Comparative costs of AC and DC transmission

Metre for metre an HVDC cable is cheaper than an HVAC cable, and has lower transmission losses. However, because the feeder and recipient networks are

AC, converter stations are required to convert AC to DC at one end and vice versa at the other, and these add an extra fixed cost to any DC line. Therefore, for short distances and networks AC is a better option, but for long distance point-to-point transmission, especially under water, HVDC is favoured. Figure 4.3.10 below shows the standard break-even analysis between AC and DC.

FIGURE 4.3.10   Standard break-even analysis between AC and DC

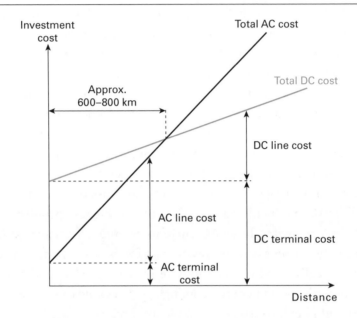

Laying an HVDC cable

The success of any interconnector relies on the design and quality of the cable and the way it is laid and protected. Each cable is optimized for a specific project's conditions, depending on whether it is to be underwater, overhead or buried underground. An overhead cable will usually be made from aluminium, as it is lighter and still has good conductivity, whereas a marine or underground cable may have a copper core, surrounded by insulation and exterior steel armour. An HVDC marine cable has the circumference of a dinner plate.

Prior to construction of the cable, a detailed seabed survey will be carried out. The cable will be tailor-made to match each section of the seabed as it changes all the way along. It will then be stored on drums for transport, and loaded onto a special ship for laying.

Most marine cables are laid in a trench and buried where possible to protect them from accidents. Finally, converter stations are built at each end to convert the AC into DC and back again. Maintenance is a serious undertaking. Faults occur at a rate in the order of 0.1 failure per year per 100 kilometres, and to repair a fault the exact location must be first identified. The cable is then floated up to the surface, repaired and re-sunk. In practice, cable-laying projects take a long time to plan, finance and gain planning and other consents. The industry rule of thumb for costs for a marine cable starts at something like US $1 million per kilometre, depending on cable type and conditions.

Alternatives to the supergrid

There are choices to be made about our future power sources. Cheap renewables from distant resources are not the only answer. For example, many proponents of green energy believe in a 'small is beautiful' world where energy production is widely distributed in small, self-sufficient communities. In this model, the role of grids is more to redistribute surplus energy, rather than provide long-distance bulk transmission. This vision would require extra investment in localized energy storage, demand-response, and energy efficiency, and less in grids.

Renewables are steadily becoming more competitive, and may one day be able to compete without subsidies. If costs fall far enough, then it may not even matter if the resource is poor if you can still harvest cheap power by deploying enough cheap generating capacity. The question is: Will the power from high quality but distant resources be cheaper, or serve us better, than power from closer poor quality resources? The answer depends on the rate of decline in the cost of transmission versus decline in the costs of renewable generation, and how this balances in the equation of better yet distant resources, as against the convenience (or even inconvenience, given planning considerations) of local ones.

For what it is worth, my prediction is that in 100 years' time we will live in a grid-connected world, and we will have abundant, cheap renewable energy. Each region will have its own supergrid, and will also have plenty of local generation. These regional grids will themselves be connected, and

Buckminster Fuller will have been proved right. And when people look back at the renewable energy revolution, I like to imagine they will say in the style of the famous *Sun* newspaper headline: 'It was the grid wot won it'.

Godfrey Spickernell has a long-standing interest in renewable energy, and is a Supergrid enthusiast. He is co-founder of Atlantic Supergrid LLP.

Further details: e-mail: **godfrey.spickernell@atlanticsupergrid.com**.

Prospects for self-generation

4.4

Jodi Huggett of 4Eco discusses the eco-friendly alternatives to mains supply.

The latest government statistics have identified a 27 per cent increase in the sales and fitting of renewable technologies over the last 12 months alone, resulting in more commercial properties than ever now utilizing sustainable solutions and over 11 per cent of total UK energy generation considered 'green'. This highlights a significant perception shift, with consumers and businesses alike recognizing the impact of renewables and proactively looking towards the latest developments and solutions to make the most of resources.

As such, the renewables industry is changing. Designers and manufacturers of microgeneration solutions are now working to further develop technologies by investing in research to advance systems and provide even more effective solutions to generate green energy.

With utility prices rising, natural resources dwindling and strict government legislation directing the uptake of sustainable solutions, embracing clean tech is quickly becoming a top priority for organizations nationwide. This has led to a huge progression in technologies, with developers looking towards new and improved processes to further increase energy efficiencies and provide greater financial return for users.

From rainwater harvesting and biomass boilers to solar PV panels, PVT and thermal heat pumps, there is a sustainable solution for every commercial requirement, guaranteeing an eco-friendly alternative to mains supply. These technologies are resource-efficient, cost-effective and straightforward to specify and install. What's more, with recent developments dramatically improving the systems and government loans offsetting installation costs, businesses nationwide are beginning to recognize the benefits of substituting mains supply with renewables.

However, although eco-technologies generate a significant amount of free power, many systems, such as PV panels, work at highest capacity during certain times of the day. This means that making the most of renewable resources is essential to maximize the financial benefits of installation.

Self-consumption technologies

Over the last few years, clean tech manufacturers have been looking towards new and innovative ways to progress technologies even further – as part of continued efforts to maximize the impact of sustainability. As well as energy farms and storage batteries, one area developing particularly fast is the idea of self-consumption.

Although a relatively new concept, the principle of self-consumption is simple. By diverting electricity generated from microgeneration systems directly to where it's needed most, it is possible to use green energy in more efficient ways – thus maximizing the impact of power generation and directly influencing returns.

Whether the priority is heating, lighting, daily running of equipment or monitoring appliances, identifying and prioritizing where green energy is used can provide dramatic results.

A select number of systems, like 4Eco's immerSUN, are taking the idea of self-consumption further by fully automating the process and giving users the opportunity to use 100 per cent of green energy without any manual involvement.

The immerSUN – A professional solution for self-consumption

Working in tandem with microgeneration systems, the immerSUN sends power to element-driven heating devices to ensure that surplus power is effectively utilized, rather than being exported to the grid.

As well as minimizing utility costs and increasing the efficiency of clean tech, the clever unit autonomously prioritizes power use and sends renewable energy to where it's needed most. Users simply fit, forget and save energy!

The unit is simple to operate, compatible with all generation devices and uses virtually no power to run. Furthermore, the device can be programmed to run completely automatically, using timers to effectively manage green energy.

By using systems such as the immerSUN, it is possible to maximize the impact of embracing renewables while significantly reducing reliance on mains supply and minimizing utility costs. This really is the future of self-generation and will no doubt become a key part of corporate energy strategies over the next few years.

FIGURE 4.4.1   Effectively utilizing self-generated energy – immerSUN

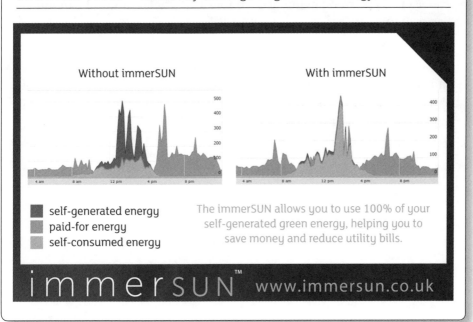

Clean efficiencies

Although self-generating energy is important, we must go further – not only to introduce self-generation technologies, but also to effectively utilize this energy. With energy preservation such a key national priority, embracing sustainability and minimizing non-renewable energy use is quickly becoming the only surefire way to alleviate utility price hikes and reduce energy bills.

Although green technologies will further develop over the next few years, the logical solution still lies with efficiency – especially the efficiency of consumption. Low-cost, effective and viable, self-consumption should be a key consideration in any corporate energy strategy.

Jodi Huggett is the Director of 4Eco, one of the UK's fastest-growing sustainable technology providers. An expert on sustainable solutions, environmental developments and clean technology, Jodi is a thought leader in eco matters, bylining 27 published articles in just 12 months.

In 2012, 4Eco's team of skilled electronic engineers developed the immerSUN – a revolutionary device that ensures effective self-consumption of green energy to significantly lower carbon emissions and improve energy efficiency levels. In just 12 months, over 11,000 units have been manufactured and distributed across the UK, prompting the design and development of a next generation unit that was launched in November 2013.

Pumped storage hydropower

Catherine Anderson at AECOM looks at the potential of a technique that meets the challenges of storing electricity and balancing the grid.

Pumped storage hydropower (PSH) schemes are one of the unknown wonders of the energy industry. They are a way of storing electricity by turning electrical energy into stored (or potential) energy and back again. Technologically well-proven, traditional PSH schemes require an upper and lower reservoir – or headpond and tailpond – which are connected by a pipeline/penstock, which in turn has a turbine connected to a reversible hydro-turbine.

The system exploits the daily variation in electrical supply and demand by pumping water from the lower reservoir to a higher reservoir during periods of low electrical demand and low prices or when other forms of electricity are providing excess capacity. The water is then released back to the lower reservoir via the penstock and hydro-turbine to generate electricity to meet sudden peaks in consumer demand or address shortfalls of capacity generated by other technologies. This cycle of pumping, storing and generating provides a flexible and valuable balancing service to the National Grid as it uses energy generated at night when electrical demand is low and can be used at very short notice during the day and other periods of peak demand. Some PSH schemes are operated to help balance peak loads but others are used as a STOR (short-term operating reserve), providing a fast response to short-term rapid changes in power demand or sudden loss in baseload supply.

AECOM

THIS IS **A KETTLE BOILING**

Using the energy from falling and flowing water, in a world of finite resources.

www.aecom.com

One of the key features for the future of PSH is in parallel to the increase of renewables; as the capacity of renewable energy increases, the need for balancing plants such as pumped storage becomes stronger. Indeed, matching consumer demand when there is increasing reliance on intermittent renewable energy, such as windfarms, means that the energy can be effectively stored with PSH schemes – making them perfect partners.

Most PSH schemes in the UK are located in Wales and Scotland. The most well known PSH scheme is Dinorwig, located in Snowdonia National Park in North Wales, which is the largest scheme of its kind in Europe (at 1728 megawatts) and has become a very popular tourist attraction known as Electric Mountain. Construction began in 1974 and it took 10 years to complete. Estimated at £425 million, it was the largest civil engineering contract ever awarded by the UK government at the time. The build involved the removal of 12 million tonnes of rock from within the Elidir Mountain in order to construct 6 kilometres of underground tunnels and an enormous cavern 51 metres tall, 180 metres long, and 23 metres wide to house the turbine hall. With all generating units operating the scheme can get to full generating capacity in approximately 16 seconds, and once running, the station can provide power for up to 6 hours before running out of water.

Other notable schemes in the UK include Ffestiniog Power Station (also in North Wales) which was the first ever built in the UK in 1963 and is capable of generating up to 360 megawatts, and Cruachan (400 megawatts) on the shores of Loch Awe in Argyll and Bute which was the world's first reversible high head PSH scheme.

In terms of the future for PSH developments in the UK, the 49-megawatt Glyn Rhonwy scheme developed by Quarry Battery Company, was the first PSH scheme to be granted permission in England and Wales in 30 years. AECOM was the principal engineering and environmental consultant on the scheme and supported Quarry Battery Company through the preliminary design, Environmental Impact Assessment (EIA), and planning process. The scheme was successfully awarded planning permission in September 2013.

Elsewhere Iberdrola/Scottish Power is currently undertaking studies to investigate the potential to increasing the size of the underground reservoir at Cruachan which could increase the capacity of the scheme to 1040 megawatts. Scottish and Southern Energy (SSE) is looking to convert the conventional hydroelectric scheme at Sloy on the shore of Loch Lomond into a PSH scheme. Furthermore SSE has recently gained planning consents for a scheme at Coire Glas (300 to 600 megawatts) on the shore of Loch Lochy, and is developing a scheme at Balmacaan (300 to 600 megawatts) on the shores of Loch Ness.

The application of PSH in other parts of the world can be much larger. Bath County in the United States is the largest PSH scheme in the world at 3003 megawatts and there are two plants located in China each with an installed capacity of 2400 megawatts.

Schemes in the UK are cleverly landscaped and make best use of their surrounding environment and topography. The penstocks and turbine hall at Dinorwig were constructed within the mountain, and the headpond, which has recently been extended, is inconspicuous in the surrounding environment. Consideration had to be given to the Arctic Char present in Llyn Peris (the water body used as the tailpond), which required the construction of a 3-kilometre diversion of the watercourse around the tailpond to enable unimpeded passage during the Char's migration. By contrast, the Glyn Rhonwy scheme is unique as it uses existing but redundant slate quarries for both headpond and tailpond.

The main factors used to identify suitable PSH sites are the level of head (ie the difference in height between the upper and lower reservoirs); the distance over which this is achieved; the topography needs to be right with redundant quarries and deep valleys that can be dammed being preferable and the existence of proximate or connected water bodies. Therefore, the locations of existing PSH schemes within the UK are primarily based on topography and landscape features and whether the engineering practicalities are possible. The Dinorwig, Ffestiniog and Sloy schemes are all located within National Parks. The existing Sloy scheme has a number of Grade I listed buildings on it and Glyn Rhonwy is located within an historic landscape. These are therefore excellent examples of how energy schemes can work within designated areas and complement the existing environmental and social landscape.

PSH technology has evolved to coastal schemes using seawater. Coastal PSH uses the same principles as traditional PSH schemes but the sea is the tailpond and therefore has to be specifically engineered to cope with these conditions. At Okinawa Island on the north-eastern coast of Japan, the headpond is lined to avoid sea-water leakage and contains secondary drainage and pumps combined with detectors to alert operators of suspected leaks. It uses fibreglass-reinforced plastic (FRP) for the penstock and the turbine is made from austenite stainless steel to minimize corrosion from the seawater and also to minimize adhesion to the equipment by marine creatures. Furthermore, the discharge outlet is located in an area with the least coral development and a breakwater was created to limit the discharge velocity to approximately 10 centimetres per second to help protect the marine environment.

Whilst environmental constraints are obviously important to the feasibility of PSH schemes, commerciality is the defining factor. The economics for PSH can be long-term and complex and there is not currently an 'off-the-shelf' cost model which is able to assess the feasibility of proposed PSH schemes, although AECOM and Quarry Battery Company are currently developing one in conjunction with DECC. In addition, they are considered large capital investments and generally the development cannot be staged. The cost of building the Glyn Rhonwy scheme is expected to be in the region of £120 million with the press reporting the cost of the proposed Cruachan extension to be in the region of £1 billion. It is also estimated that sea water PSH schemes generally cost 20 per cent more than traditional PSH schemes due to the mitigation measures needed due to the use of sea water. However, given Iberdrola has just completed a £1 billion extension to the La Muela PSH scheme in Valencia, Spain after a seven-year construction period, there is obviously some appetite for such a construction and engineering feat.

Another key element for the future of PSH is balancing the difference between off-peak and peak energy prices and this can influence the requirement for larger schemes against the utilization of a series of smaller schemes.

Finally, the growth in the potential for PSH has been equalled in part by the requirement for political support. Scottish planning policy has already recognized the potential for an expansion in pumped storage facilities within the draft National Planning Framework.

The number of operational and consented PSH schemes currently located within the UK is a clear indication that these schemes are possible within challenging environmental constraints. The relatively flexible deployment of PSH together with the proven technology at its heart, whether traditional or sea-water, can unlock both UK and worldwide potential, especially where energy generation, energy security and balancing potential are limited. It is also apparent that PSH is seen as a key companion to the increasing capacity of renewable energy schemes, such as wind farms, across the UK. Therefore, just as wind farm schemes are allocated within planning policy, so should

PSH (although it is recognized that not all parts of the UK lend themselves to the topographical requirements of a PSH scheme). With that in mind, a key function of PSH is to balance the grid. Is location really an issue or does more need to be investigated into the benefit of having a fewer number of larger schemes or a series of smaller, more localized schemes? Regardless of the size or location, the increase in awareness and recognition that it plays an important part in regulating the energy supply within the UK will no doubt make the energy, engineering and hydropower industry get increasingly excited over what feasible schemes will be brought forward.

Catherine Anderson is Associate Director at AECOM and EIA Project Manager for the Glyn Rhonwy PSH. Catherine is based in Cardiff, Bristol and Edinburgh and can be contacted on 02920 654600 or 07780 700531.

Carbon capture and storage

Judith Shapiro at the Carbon Capture & Storage Association (CSSA) reviews the emergence of a technology that is assuming a lead role in cutting carbon.

Since 2010, so much has changed in carbon capture and storage (CSS) that it's fair to say that the industry has gone through an almost complete re-birth. One aspect however, remains as true as ever – the importance of CCS.

The International Energy Agency's Energy Technology Perspectives now estimates that to reach the 2 degrees scenario (limiting global temperature increase to 2 degrees centigrade by 2050), CCS needs to contribute 17 per cent of emissions reductions in 2050 and 14 per cent of cumulative emissions reductions between 2015 and 2050. And recently, the Intergovernmental Panel on Climate Change (IPCC) Working Group 3 published their contribution to the IPCC Fifth Assessment Report on options for mitigating climate change, in which they concluded that without CCS, the costs of meeting a global goal of 450 parts per million (ppm) atmospheric concentration of CO_2 by 2100 would increase by 138 per cent!

Closer to home, the Energy Technologies Institute concludes that the cost of delivering a UK low-carbon energy mix in 2050 without CCS, would increase by £30 to £40 billion per year, or 1 per cent of gross domestic product (GDP). It is not an understatement to say that tackling climate change will be significantly more expensive if CCS is not available.

Projects update

Looking back to 2010, the UK was committed to supporting four CCS projects, with a competition for the first of these looking set to select either the Scottish Power Longannet project or the E.ON Kingsnorth project. In the end, E.ON pulled out and the negotiations on the Longannet project were unsuccessful, so the entire competition was abandoned. However, one must applaud the Government at the time for its quick response – a new, re-vamped CCS competition was launched in April 2012 (as part of the CCS Roadmap which was published at the same time). This competition was named the 'CCS Commercialization Programme' to signify that the focus is now on delivering the outcome; fossil fuel power stations with CCS able to be cost-competitive with other low-carbon technologies in the 2020s under the new Electricity Market Reform framework.

Out of the eight bids that came forward, the Government selected its two preferred bidders in March 2013. These are the White Rose coal-CCS project on the Drax site in Yorkshire and the Shell/SSE gas-CCS project at Peterhead in Scotland. Both of these projects have now successfully signed contracts to progress to Front End Engineering Design studies, and it is estimated that these studies should take approximately 18 months, with final investment decisions expected (if all goes well) towards the end of 2015 or beginning of 2016. In another positive sign of progress, as part of the White Rose project, National Grid will be developing the 'Yorkshire Humber CCS Trunkline' – a pipeline able to transport a large amount of CO_2 from a number of power and industrial emitters. Once this pipeline is in operation, it will signal the birth of a CCS cluster in the Yorkshire/Humber region – this will play a major role in the cost-effective decarbonization of both power and industrial sectors in one of the highest-emitting regions in the UK.

Looking beyond the UK, the global CCS picture is actually fairly positive. In its 2014 Global Status of CCS report, the Global CCS Institute identifies 12 large-scale CCS projects in operation around the world and another nine in construction. Crucially, of these nine projects, the first two CCS projects on a coal-fired power station are due to begin operation in 2014 – in Canada and the US – and these two projects will provide valuable lessons for other countries seeking to decarbonize fossil fuels with CCS.

Whilst CCS plays an important role in decarbonizing the power sector, it is also becoming increasingly apparent that CCS is a vital technology for many industrial sectors such as steel, cement, chemicals and refining. Due to the fact that the CO_2 emissions from these sectors is process as well as fuel-generated, CCS is actually the only decarbonization option available that can deliver deep cuts in industrial emissions. Although the development of policies to stimulate industrial CCS in the UK has so far not been forthcoming, the Government did give some consideration to this issue in December 2013, when they announced that funding would be made available towards an industrial CCS feasibility study as part of the Tees Valley City Deal. This City Deal represents an agreement reached between the UK Government and Teesside to help boost process industries in the region – creating a large number of jobs and unlocking private-sector investment.

Costs and funding

One of the most significant pieces of work on CCS to be published in the UK in the last few years is the CCS Cost Reduction Task Force final report – published in May 2013. The Task Force was established in 2012 to identify opportunities for cost reduction across the CCS chain to achieve cost competitive CCS in the 2020s. The main conclusion of the report states that:

> UK gas and coal power stations equipped with carbon capture, transport and storage have clear potential to be cost-competitive with other forms of low-carbon power generation, delivering electricity at a levelised cost approaching £100/MWh by the early 2020s, and at a cost significantly below £100/MWh soon thereafter.

Of the various aspects of CCS that contribute to this cost reduction pathway, by far the most significant is the ability to share CCS transport and storage infrastructure – this will not only deliver future CCS power projects at considerably lower cost, but will also be vital to enable cost-effective decarbonization of industrial sectors (as mentioned earlier).

The UK has spent many years considering how best to support CCS projects. Back in 2010, a dedicated CCS incentive was introduced – a levy on electricity suppliers to fund CCS projects. However, this incentive was scrapped when the coalition government came into power. Instead, the current government embarked on a much bigger task – the introduction of electricity market reform (EMR). This can be considered as the most significant overhaul of the electricity market since privatization and has at its core the three aims of a secure, low-carbon and affordable electricity system for the UK – made up of nuclear, renewables and fossil fuels with CCS. The cornerstone mechanism within EMR is the Feed-in Tariff Contract for Difference (FiT CfD) –

this is a world first for CCS as it provides an ongoing incentive able to support CCS beyond demonstration projects.

Conclusion

In summary, although there have been many changes since 2010, there is still much to be positive about in the CCS industry. The CCSA and the Trades Union Congress (TUC) recently published a joint report on 'The Economic Benefits of CCS in the UK', in which it is estimated that CCS can created 15,000–30,000 jobs annually by 2030, with a cumulative market value of £15 to £35 billion by the same date. Once the first UK CCS projects begin operating, the UK will reap the benefits of this exciting new industry and will take its place amongst the global 'club' of countries that are at the forefront of the vital technology.

Judith Shapiro joined the Carbon Capture & Storage Association in September 2006 to support the Association's activities in CCS policy and communications, and represents the interests of the CCSA members in promoting the business of CCS. Judith has been with the Association since its launch in March 2006, and has assisted in establishing the Association to become the leading voice of the CCS industry, both in the UK and internationally, thus ensuring that CCS is now regarded as a credible low-carbon energy technology for the future.

Prior to joining CCSA, Judith worked for both the UK Business Council for Sustainable Energy and the Combined Heat and Power Association as a Researcher. Judith has a BSc in Biology and an MSc in Environmental Technology from Imperial College, London.

Further information is available from Carbon Capture & Storage Association, 10 Dean Farrar Street, London SW1H 0DX (website: **www.ccsassociation.org**).

PART FIVE
Renewable sources

De-risking ocean energy

Raymond Alcorn, **Gordon Dalton**, **Mark Healy** and **Michael O'Connor** at Beaufort Research review the potential and the risks in tidal and wave energy.

Tapping into the vast energy resource that is contained in the world's oceans has always been seen as a challenge, but one with huge potential rewards. Ocean energy developments have been driven not only by the energy resource, but also the opportunity for job creation, supply chain development as well as diversity and security of the energy mix. The total theoretical energy contained in the seas is estimated to be 32,000 terawatt hours per year (TWh/yr) for wave energy[1] and 7,800 terawatt hours per year for tides[2]. Wave energy devices derive energy from the three-dimensional movement of ocean waves. Tidal energy devices harness the bodily movement of water resulting from the environmental pull between the sun, moon and the earth. The efficiencies of future ocean energy technologies will dictate how much of this resource can be usefully (or technically) harnessed. The technically exploitable energy of wave energy devices is estimated to be 5,500 terawatt hours per year[3], which is approximately 30 per cent of the world's electricity demand.

The enormous exploitable energy available in the oceans indicates that there is significant market potential for wave and tidal energy devices as well as opportunities for the supporting industries involved in the development, manufacturing, construction, installation and operation services. Owing to uncertain future costs of generation, estimates of the long-term market size of wave and tidal energy tend to be approximate. However, the World Energy Council estimates the global capital expenditure for wave energy projects to be more than £500 billion, based on a technically exploitable wave resource of 2,000 terawatt hours per year.[4]

The enormous potential supply of ocean energy is matched by significant drivers on the demand side. As well as offering an alternative to fossil fuels, ocean energy offers technical and geographical diversification to other renewable energy sources as well as greater predictability. Tidal energy is predictable up to 100 years in advance, while wave energy is highly predictable days in advance and complements wind energy by generally achieving its peak energy after wind energy has reached its maximum. This makes ocean energy attractive to grid operators by adding more predictable and consistent sources of renewable energy, which has the effect of smoothing out the overall power supply from renewables thereby reducing the reliance on conventional plant.

Ocean energy is not yet commercial and technologies are still in developmental phase. Wave energy has many concepts under development, however unlike wind energy, designs for wave energy devices have not yet converged to a 'standard' technology solution. There is more than one solution for extraction of energy and it is likely that different solutions will be more economically suited to different locations or resource types. Currently there are approximately 70 wave energy design concepts currently under development, a few of which have made it to full-scale prototype testing. There are some near-commercial devices but no arrays, although the first small arrays are planned for 2017. For tidal energy, there appears to be more technological convergence of the technologies, with several developers testing full-scale prototypes and plans for many commercial deployments.

An important recent milestone has been a number of large engineering entities taking controlling stakes in device development companies, primarily in tidal technology companies, indicating that the tidal industry is closer to maturity than wave. These companies include Siemens, DCNS, Andriz Hydro, Alstom and others. In the last seven years up to 2014, total private-sector investment in the industry has been over 600 million euros in Europe.[5]

Complementing private-sector interest in ocean energy is strong government support for the industry. Countries such as the UK and Ireland are offering significant support to their ocean energy industries, with five renewable obligation certificates (ROCs)[6] available for UK deployments and Ireland recently promising 0.26 euro per kilowatt-hour (kWh) for the first 30 megawatts deployed.[7] There is also support at European level where the EU's 80-billion euro Horizon 2020 work programme contains calls for ocean energy initiatives in the fields of research, innovation and demonstration. Tidal energy projects have also been successful in achieving funding for demonstration projects under the NER300[8] programme. Based on the anticipated commercialization of the industry, there are over 2 gigawatts of ocean energy projects in the planning pipelines of Europe's largest utilities, with over 40 wave and tidal sites leased already in the UK by the Crown Estate.[5]

Current issues facing the industry – technical and non-technical barriers

Why hasn't the wave and tidal industry established itself as a competing renewable energy technology after up to 40 years of research and development undertaken since the 1970s?[9] The contributing ingredients to the delay in consolidation of the sector are many-fold. Wave energy development has been hampered by a lack of confidence in current existing technology concepts. It has been questioned how so many wave energy companies move all the way through the TRLs (Technology Readiness Levels),[10] reaching pre-commercial scale, and fail. The recommended rigorous application of the TRL design and testing regime appears not to be adhered to. Funding and investor pressures unique to this sector are most probably the main culprits, with additional pressures from government funding contract structures rewarding megawatt-per-hour (MWh) production rather than robust designs. More stringent concept evaluation, driven centrally by government funding bodies and investors at early stage development would eliminate most weak design concepts.

Tidal technology development is moving to the final TRL of pre-commercial demonstrations, raising the confidence levels in that sector substantially. Tidal technologies are now being tested at pre-commercial phase via private and FP7/NER300 project-funding mechanisms, with progress proceeding on schedule, with relatively few technical setbacks.

Despite the recent progress in the tidal sector, like wave, there are no commercial arrays of wave or tidal devices in the water, demonstrating that neither technology currently has the technical capacity to generate reliably at present. This lack of confidence in wave energy technology development in particular is reflected by the recent closures of some longstanding wave development companies. Two major NER300 projects for wave demonstration have also been postponed.

Investor insecurity in wave energy has been compounded by the lack of sustained government and regulatory policy support. Whilst governments like Denmark have trail-blazed exemplar support policies to ignite the Danish wind energy experience,[11] similar inspirational policy supporting wave energy has failed to materialise. Governments are simply not as supportive to wave energy technologies as they have been to their wind energy counterparts. The support mechanisms lacking are twofold. The first gap is in the range of grants available, which are usually limited to 50 per cent funding or conditional on achieving certain targets, resulting in the high-risk companies failing to secure the grants. The Danish experience offered up to 80 per cent finance grants and should be replicated by wave energy funding bodies. Furthermore, the Danish government commissioned the Danish utilities to install the first offshore wind demonstrator projects, providing the regulatory drive to successfully develop the technology. The government support mechanism promising future revenue such as feed-in tariffs/ROCs or the UK Marine Renewables Deployment Fund (MRDF) are only beneficial in stimulating investment when the technologies are at TRL9. These have benefited tidal developments to some extent, and but not wave at all. The advertised tariffs for wave energy could be viewed as theoretical only, as the funds allocated have never been drawn down to date. Moreover, many studies for wave energy financial viability have stated that current tariff supports are inadequate, and need to be at least over 0.30 euro per kilowatt-hour, such as the UK-ROCs scheme, to be financially viable.[12] Ultimately, the funding mechanisms need to be streamlined and dovetailed with the TRLs and the companies developing the technology need to develop their business alongside their technology development.

Finally, the necessary infrastructure investments that are needed, such as reinforcing electrical grid networks and upgrading of ports required for the roll-out of large-scale ocean renewables are still many years from materializing[13] Investors see that most sites of high ocean renewable potential are remote from population centres, with inadequate current plans for upgrading facilities to the scale of development planned. Investor confidence will be significantly boosted if it sees major government funding to upgrade infrastructures at this current time, providing the ingredients for successful future technology roll-out, supply chain development and job creation.

De-risking the industry

Risk in ocean energy is made up of uncertainty and impact, and an understanding of both is required. Evaluating risk is therefore key for technology developers, site developers, investors and government alike when considering investment in the ocean energy industry at present. Risk appears at every level – in determining energy output and cost, technology/company valuation, government support mechanisms etc. Most of the risks trace back to the basic technology – its development, effectiveness and reliability – and hence the cost of the energy ultimately produced. The industry recognizes that this is the problem area and steps are actively being taken to reduce risks to acceptable levels.

In the first instance, there is now significant underpinning of technology development. Resource data, critical for location-specific technology design, are now more widely available. Techno-economic decision support tools specific to ocean energy have now been developed, such as Navitas[14] and Energinet.[15] Parallel to this is the emergence of world-class ocean energy test centres and research centres (such as Beaufort Research[16] and Narec[17]) with associated expertise at every scale. These provide support facilities for small-scale concept testing in wave tanks all the way through to full-scale pre-commercial testing at ocean test sites. Europe is leading the way on this front, having developed a full suite of world-class ocean energy test centres and hosting the highest concentration of leading experts in the field. The United States, Canada, Australia, China, Japan and Taiwan, for example do not have such a comprehensive or advanced array of test infrastructure and expertise and are looking to Europe as the leader in the field. The European Commission has sought to build on and integrate this European marine energy infrastructure and expertise through establishing a formal network of this test infrastructure called MARINET.[18] This encourages and facilitates ocean energy technology development through providing funded access to these test centres.

Both investors and developers of ocean technologies are beginning to realize the value of staged technology development rather than the foolhardy approach of moving too quickly to develop a full-scale ocean-going device. The Ocean Energy Systems framework of the International Energy Association (IEA)[19] has endorsed a five-stage structured development path for the technical and economic development of ocean energy technologies from concept through to commercial arrays. This path details exactly what needs to be tested and achieved at each stage before a technology should move on to the next level and is directly linked to the wider TRL concept that is used for assessing general technology development progress. International standards, such as those developed by EquiMar,[20] are now being progressed via the IEC[21] for global adoption as the first international standards for marine renewable energy. Certification bodies such as DNV GL[22] and BV,[23] who are trusted authorities to carry out verification work in the marine sector, have set up ocean energy-specific divisions. These are using the above standards in order to approve and authorise a technology to progress through the stages of development or to independently verify the extent of development and effectiveness of an ocean energy technology. This provides technical confidence for potential investors, partners or funding agencies as well as a mechanism by which to compare technologies like-for-like.

The wise marine energy investor or partner should therefore look for certified evidence of adherence to these standards as a minimum criterion prior to getting involved. All those in the industry, particularly investors and potential partners, need to adopt this rigorous approach to standards of technology development. This requires investor knowledge of the industry so that expectations can be sensible in terms of development time frames and costs. As we have seen, without this approach, failures are inevitable and development time, costs and risks rise exponentially. Universal adoption of this certified standards approach on the other hand significantly reduces risks and provides clearer delineation when it comes to apportioning risks.

Conclusion

What should an investor conclude about investment in ocean energy technologies in 2014? It seems increasingly obvious that the fortunes of tidal and wave energy have diverged at the present time. Tidal technology development is emerging onto the final TRL stage of proto-type testing, with a number of successful designs and a number of large entities now willing to invest in those companies. Tidal energy seems certain to be technically viable, and in time should become commercially viable, albeit with a much smaller global resource than wave energy. Wave energy, although much larger in potential, has no pre-commercial arrays in the water, but this should not signal that wave energy is not technically or commercially viable.

This article has detailed that a number of crucial background support structures have recently been implemented that have significantly improved the current stage of wave energy technology development. These include a number of new world-class research infrastructures that have been recently funded, a new range of bespoke software decision tools and most importantly, an endorsed and now universally-implemented set of standards and stage design protocols. All these recent mechanisms should ensure that new emerging wave energy designs will have a much higher chance of progressing to successful commercial scale deployment.

The resource has been measured, the opportunity is well understood and we know that the energy can be efficiently converted. We also now know much better how to evaluate the technology, the associated business plan and how to quantify risk in terms of uncertainty and impact. Through developing standards, guidelines and best practice we can also now equitably compare technologies and projects and understand where time, money and effort should best be focused in order to create a commercial technology.

We also see that, mirroring other industries, strong confidence of where technologies are on a TRL scale gives different categories of investors specific entry and exit points along the development pathway. The EU has also signalled this, with a portfolio of financial opportunities for the sector that are all based around adherence and development to TRLs.

The new investor should now have more confidence that investments in emerging ocean-energy technologies will now produce a return on investment, provided that they take the time to invest responsibly.

Dr Raymond Alcorn is one of the Directors of Beaufort Research. In this role he has assisted government with ocean energy support mechanisms as well as helping companies to find development finance.

Dr Gordon Dalton is an ocean energy economics engineer at Beaufort Research and is project manager for the Navitas techno-economic software development.

Mark Healy is a project manager at Beaufort Research. He conducts technical and commercial evaluations of ocean energy companies and leads MARINET, the European marine renewables infrastructure network.

Michael O'Connor is a research engineer at Beaufort Research and is technical lead on the Navitas techno-financial software commercialisation project.

Beaufort Research, University College Cork, is Ireland's leading marine research centre, supporting development and innovation in the maritime and energy fields.

Further details: tel: 021 425 0021; e-mail: **beaufortresearch@ucc.ie**; Twitter: **@beaufortucc**; website: **www.beaufortresearch.ie.**

Notes

1 Mork, G, Barstow, S, Kabuth, A and Pontes, M T (2010) Assessing the global wave energy potential, in Proc of 29th International Conference on Ocean, Offshore and Arctic Engineering, ASME, paper, 2010.

2 IEA-OES (2011) An international vision for ocean energy.

3 Lewis, A, Estefen, S, Huckerby, J, Musial, W, Pontes, T and Torres-Martinez, J (2011) Ocean Energy.

4 World Energy Council (2007) Survey of energy sources [Online] http://www.worldenergy.org/wec-geis/publications/reports/ser04/overview.asp.

5 EU-OEA (2013) European Ocean Energy – Industry vision paper.

6 https://www.ofgem.gov.uk/environmental-programmes/renewables-obligation-ro

7 ReNews (2014) Dublin Sweetens Ocean Waters, [Online] http://renews.biz/60168/dublin-sweetens-ocean-waters.

8 NER300 is a financing instrument managed jointly by the European Commission, European Investment Bank and Member States.

9 Dalton, G J (2010) Why Wave Energy – Market driver analysis for investors and policy makers, OES-IA 2010 [Online] http://www.ocean-energy-systems.org/library/annual_reports/

10 Technology Readiness Level: www.westwave.ie/wp-content/uploads/downloads/2012/10/Wave-Power-Systems-Technology-Readiness-Definition-ESBIoe-WAV-12-091-Rev2.pdf

11 Dalton, G and Gallachóir, B P Ó (2010) Building a wave energy policy focusing on innovation, manufacturing and deployment, *Renewable and Sustainable Energy Reviews*, **14**, pp 2339–58.

12 Teillant, B, Costello, R, Weber, J and Ringwood, J (2012) Productivity and economic assessment of wave energy projects through operational simulations, *Renewable Energy*, 48, pp 220–30.

13 Intelligent Energy Europe (IEA), 'Waveplam,' 2010, [Online] http://www.waveplam.eu/files/downloads/D.3.2.Guidelienes_FINAL.pdf.

14 www.ucc.ie/en/hmrc/projects/navitas.

15 www.juliafchozas.com/projects/coe-calculation-tool.

16 www.ucc.ie/beaufort.

17 www.narec.co.uk.

18 MARINET – Marine Renewables Infrastructure Network, funded by the European Commission under FP7 (www.fp7-marinet.eu).

19 IEA-OES – International Energy Agency Ocean Energy Systems (www.ocean-energy-systems.org).

20 EquiMar – initiative funded by the European Commission to deliver a suite of protocols for the equitable evaluation of marine energy converters (www.equimar.org).

21 IEC – International Electrotechnical Commission (www.iec.ch).

22 DNV GL (www.dnvgl.com).

23 BV (www.bureauveritas.com/wps/wcm/connect/bv_com/group).

Solar technology

Lee Sutton, Director at 4Eco, discusses the latest developments in solar technology – from self-generation and fiscal return to feed-in tariffs and self-consumption.

O ver the last decade, solar technology has developed significantly. From commercial photovoltaics and solar farms to photovoltaic (PVT) and solar thermal set-ups, there is now an energy-efficient alternative to suit every requirement; capable of saving money, reducing reliance on mains supply and minimizing carbon emissions.

But with rising energy costs and an increasing number of international regulations guiding corporate commitment to sustainability, embracing sustainable solutions is becoming essential. This has made understanding the latest advances and range of technologies available fundamental to making informed corporate energy investments.

The state of solar technology

Despite slow early development and cautious uptake, it seems that the solar energy world is changing. Renewables are becoming increasingly common-place and the efficiency of technology is progressing on a daily basis.

According to energy research expert and solar academic, David Elliott, solar power is the next big step in resource consumption and will play a key part in solving the global energy crisis. 'Globally there is over 100 gigawatts (GW) of PV in use, and its adoption is accelerating as investment costs fall,' explains David. He goes on to state:

In the UK alone we generate over 2.3 gigawatts of green energy every year, which will reach 10 gigawatts by 2050 if current pickup rates continue.

This amounts to over 25 per cent of our entire annual energy usage figures – a monumental figure.

But this is only the start. Worldwide figures have already reached 100 gigawatts, with targets expecting to see this increase significantly over the next decade. If predictions are correct, this would mean that, in just 30 years, energy generated via solar PV could outweigh energy produced from coal.

In business terms, this means that practices are changing and technologies are progressing rapidly, providing a huge opportunity to organizations globally. Corporate annual energy bills can reach thousands, if not millions of pounds – but this could all change by embracing efficient and cost-effective technology. Not only does solar provide a free, renewable source of natural energy, but with generation system prices dropping considerably and government support for financial investment a worthwhile incentive, making the step to sustainability is the sensible solution.

The development of solar technology

Commercial photovoltaic systems have been around for over 100 years, but today's high-efficiency systems have only become popular since 1970 – and a worthwhile alternative to mains supply in the last decade.

From humble beginnings as small low-wattage single cells, present-day next-generation solar systems are used to generate electricity for a multitude of uses: from pumping water, substituting domestic power, charging batteries, supplying power to the national grid and even power space exploration vehicles. What's more, the technology has limitless up-scaling potential if specified correctly and can almost eliminate utility bills in many circumstances.

But what types of solar technology are available? And which are the most effective for substituting non-renewable resources? An outline follows of the most common solar technologies – solar photovoltaics and solar thermal – as well as their uses in a corporate setting.

Solar PV

Solar panel systems, also known as solar photovoltaics (PV), capture the sun's energy using specialist electrical cells. As light hits the cells, sunlight intensity is immediately converted into electricity, which can be used in substitution for energy previously bought-in from the national grid.

From powering the entire lighting of multi-million square-foot warehouses to driving international computer server equipment and even generating power for electronic road signs, the potential for solar PV in a commercial capacity is vast.

In some circumstances PV panels have even been combined to create large-scale 'farms', covering huge areas of unused land. These farms generate enormous amounts of solar energy, which can be used for large-scale electrical supply. In fact, a farm the size of Derbyshire could generate the UK's entire electricity requirements for a whole year!

Solar thermal

Unlike solar PV, solar thermal captures and collects thermal energy from sunlight. This energy is used to heat water, which can then be applied in a number of commercial and domestic functions.

Although more limited in application than solar PV, solar thermal can capture huge amounts of energy throughout the year, and be used for traditionally costly purposes. From heating Olympic swimming pools and running electric power generation to providing hot water and central heating for office buildings, solar thermal is a highly efficient solar technology.

So, regardless of energy requirements, scale or application, there is a solar solution perfect for you.

Using solar tech to break eco boundaries

As the owner and self-builder of one of the UK's most environmentally friendly eco developments, architect Richard Hawkes is committed to embracing the latest sustainable design solutions.

'Crossway', an extraordinary green development situated in the heart of rural Kent, is one of Richard's finest architectural achievements and boasts some of the most innovative carbon cutting technologies available.

Costing less than £400 to run every year, the project demonstrates the potential of sustainability and highlights how prioritizing solar technologies can provide a reliable and efficient alternative to deliver entire energy requirements.

The project's 4.5 kW PV array is complimented with a 3.4 kW PV-T system, while an immerSUN microgen controller is used to direct excess electricity to element-driven heating devices – minimizing reliance on non-renewables resources and eliminating heating bills.

Awarded PassivHaus status and numerous international awards, Crossway is a beacon for eco friendly alternatives and highlights the potential of solar tech.

Expectations for the future

Solar technology is quickly becoming the most effective solution to combating high energy costs, meeting international environmental targets and protecting natural resources. What's more, with huge recent technological developments, financial initiatives and green loans to offset investment costs, now is the perfect time to embrace commercial potential.

But low-carbon can't stop there. Sustainability is everyone's business and we must all play our part. Government support is essential, but so is the backing of corporations, local businesses, homeowners and individuals, who must all work together to push forward for a greener future. By looking towards the latest green products, we can all play our part in pushing forward technology and minimizing the environmental impact of our corporate activity.

Lee Sutton is the Technical Director of 4Eco-immerSUN, the UK's leading supplier and manufacturer of surplus microgen energy controllers. An expert in electronic product design and development, Lee has worked in the renewables sector for a number of years, helping homeowners and businesses to embrace green technologies and reduce carbon emissions. Before setting up 4Eco, Lee spearheaded a specialist solar tech firm, installing eco technologies into homes and businesses across the country, but in 2012 made the decision to move away from installations and instead focus on the research and development of solar tech. Working with a team of electrical engineers, Lee created a solution to increase the efficiencies of solar PV even further – the immerSUN. A multi-purpose microgeneration switching device, the immerSUN directs excess green energy to element-driven heating devices – reducing utility costs significantly and eliminating the requirement for energy storage.

Offshore renewable energy

Nick Medic, Director of offshore renewables at RenewableUK asks:

Has the future arrived?

In his 1976 book *The Next 200 Years* futurologist Herman Kahn notes that 'offshore locations are now being considered seriously for large energy installations.' What seemed to be the distant future at the time has now become a reality. Following the success of the United Kingdom's initial rounds of offshore wind energy development, starting with the installation of the first wind turbines off the coast of Blyth in 2002, the plans for a further build out have significantly expanded.

In January 2010 The Crown Estate, the manager of the seabed within the UK's 'Exclusive Economic Zone' (EEZ) announced the start of a leasing round for sites covering a total of around 25,000 km² and the potential to accommodate over 30 gigawatts of capacity. The so-called Round 3 leasing programme in conjunction with the earlier Rounds 1 and 2, could add around 45 gigawatts of electricity generating capacity to the UK, providing around 40 per cent of the nation's electricity. And in terms of potential for future development it should be noted that the United Kingdom's EEZ is 773,676 km² – meaning that only around 3 per cent of it has been so far set aside for offshore development.

However, before we go on, it is worth asking the fundamental question: Why go offshore? Going back to Mr Kahn's book and his pioneering work, grappling with the colossal question of how to secure modern societies' energy supplies is no less pressing now than it was during futurology's heyday in the 1970s and 1980s. The question is further complicated by factors such as population growth, requiring more land to be used for agriculture and

The Value of Membership

Join the UK's Leading Renewable Energy Trade Association

renewableUK
The voice of wind & marine energy

1 Grow Your Business
Membership demonstrates ambition and enables industry engagement

2 Protect Your Future
We champion your industry; your membership strengthens our voice

3 Meet the Right People
We connect hundreds of organisations and thousands of professionals

4 Achieve More
Our members make their money go further and gain a return on investment

5 Keep Up To Date
Receive information and insight to help you make informed decisions

Our vision is for renewable energy to play a leading role in powering the UK. Our members are integral to achieving this goal.

Join us and become part of the RenewableUK community. You'll be in excellent company.

To find out more, visit **www.RenewableUK.com** or contact **membership@RenewableUK.com**

housing, the depletion of conventional energy sources and, finally, capabilities of cutting-edge research and development (R&D) to resolve lingering uncertainties over the safety of nuclear energy and viability of untapped sources of energy.

Offshore wind energy seems to be able to answer all of the above challenges. Firstly, by definition it does not take up valuable space on land, and can thus be deployed close to large urban conglomerations, without having a negative socio-economic impact. This seems pertinent given public opposition to extracting natural gas by fracking and the entrenched opposition in many parts of Europe to long-term nuclear storage solutions. In other parts of the world it is often new hydro-electric projects that are the problem, flooding valuable land and necessitating large resettlement programs. For instance, the UK's 22 offshore wind farms covering around 400 km² of seabed now provide more electricity than the Aswan Dam (Lake Nasser) with a surface area of over 5,000 km². In addition, the space between the offshore turbines is still open to access and can be used for a number of purposes including recreational access.

In fact, being near to large centres of population could not only ensure offshore wind not only supplies the much required energy, but it stimulates employment growth in those areas where it is needed the most. As an example, many of the arguments around building offshore wind farms off the US east coast, despite offshore wind technology's higher costs, focus on the economic opportunity for the once thriving industrial ports in the coastal states. The 'economic tonic effect' of offshore wind has already been observed in the UK, where it has driven up employment in the sector both during construction but also in the long term, with jobs in the 20-year operations and maintenance phase of the wind farms' life cycle.

Obviously, this would be of little relevance were offshore wind farms not an effective way to produce energy. However, as we have noted above, the outputs from the UK's pool of offshore turbines can already be positively compared to more established forms of electricity generation. From a standing start in 2002, offshore wind now provides around 4 per cent of the nation's electricity share a, that is set to surpass 10 per cent in the next five years. This contribution will help offset some of the declines in indigenous energy production. For example, crude oil outputs from the UK's North Sea oilfields have dropped from 4 billion barrels in 2003 to just over 1.5 billion barrels in 2012, according to Oil and Gas UK. At the same time the UK's coal reserves covering underground and surface, at a seemingly impressive 3,196 million tonnes, would only last another 50 years if the total UK demand was satisfied out of domestic production. In both cases, fossil fuels are proving not just polluting, but increasingly scarce – and in both cases the answer so far has been to increase imports. For example, out of the 64 million tonnes of coal used in the UK in 2012, only around 15 per cent was produced domestically, with the rest covered by imports, mainly from Russia, Colombia and the US, according to UK Coal.

It is clear that offshore wind can significantly enhance the UK's energy security, and the extent becomes even clearer when we look at some of the most recent developments in scaling up the offshore turbine technology. At the moment the average capacity of an offshore turbine in UK waters is around 3.3 megawatts (MW). Given the average wind speed and availability, each turbine on average produces around 10 gigawatt-hours (GWh) of electricity. Doubling the turbines' capacity would increase the output to around 20 gigawatt-hours – and this is exactly what is currently happening in offshore turbine research and development (R&D). Samsung, Siemens, Vestas/Mitsubishi and Senvion (formerly RePower) are already building and testing 5 megawatt-plus 'superturbines', which at the top end of the scale are reaching powers of 8 megawatts. This offers some interesting perspectives on how many offshore turbines would be needed to satisfy the UK's electricity demand.

If we assume that the currently tested 8-megawatt machines would be the norm (although a recent European Commission-backed report asserted that current state of technology allows for 20-megawatt machines), and we further assume total UK electricity consumption in the long term to peak at between 310 and 320 terawatt-hours (TWh), we get an estimate of around 13,000 offshore turbines supplying all of the UK's required terawatt-hours, based on the historical load factor of 35 per cent. Can these turbines be accommodated within the UK's EEZ (exclusive economic zone)? As we have seen from the above – without a doubt! It seems that the future, which even for Herman Kahn must have seemed distant, is finally arriving.

Finally, the question is whether, in purely financial terms, offshore wind is a good bet. If other generating technologies can offer the same benefits (low-carbon emissions, energy security and economic benefits) should we not be expanding and balancing our energy portfolio, keeping a keen eye on the levelized cost of energy (LCOE)? Arguably the emphasis of the UK's Energy Act 2012 was on long-term affordability, which the legislation sought to achieve in the first instance by balancing support provisions against what the government intends to spend on supporting low-carbon generation, through the Levy Control Framework. The argument at work here is that offshore wind as the most expensive readily scalable technology needs to be reined in, to achieve best value to the consumer.

On closer examination, however, it quickly becomes obvious that this line of argument has little going for it. Offshore wind electricity costs are higher than from other conventional sources, because these are, by and large, mature technologies which have in many cases been built out of the public's purse, at a time when they were nationalized industries. There are still numerous costs to these technologies that are not included in the LCOE. For instance, the Nuclear Decommissioning Authority has spent £6.8 billion in 2010 out of departmental budget. Given that 62,000 megawatt-hours were generated in that year by the UK's nuclear power plants, for each 1 megawatt-hour of electricity generated, £109 of public money was spent on decommissioning. Including the actual price of electricity of around £50 per megawatt-hour this brings the total cost per megawatt-hour for nuclear energy to over £150. Nor is 2010 an exception with long-term spending on nuclear decommissioning hovering around £4 billion per year. The situation is unlikely to change with the government currently incentivizing nuclear with a generous guaranteed tariff over 35 years and underwriting some of the liabilities, despite the fact that the technology is over 60 years old and established across the EU.

In contrast, with little more than a decade of sector development, offshore practitioners have now committed to bringing down costs by a third in the next five years. Gradually, the costs are expected to reach £100 per mega-watt-hour by 2020 and within the next decade start moving to parity. This opens the door to a truly exciting prospect of vast offshore arrays generating plentiful, low-cost electricity with little of the attendant environmental or social drawbacks – indeed, with all the attendant socio-economic benefits. This was one of the dreams of past futurologists, and seems like it is coming to pass. Offshore wind is both the future and it is already here.

RenewableUK is the UK's leading trade and professional body for the wind and marine renewables industries. Our primary purpose is to promote the use of wind, wave and tidal power in and around the UK. We act as a central point for information for our membership and as a lobbying group to promote wind energy and marine renewables to government, industry, the media and the public. We research and find solutions to current issues and generally act as the forum for the UK wind, wave and tidal industry.

Further details: tel: 020 7901 3000; e-mail: **info@renewable-uk.com.**

Reference

Kahn, H (1976) *The Next 200 Years: A scenario for America and the world*, Morrow, New York

Biomass

You can profit from biomass, but can you handle it, asks
Professor Mike Bradley, Director of The Wolfson Centre for
Bulk Solids Handling Technology, University of Greenwich

Biomass is everywhere and there are many ways to make money out of it. Traditionally, you could burn it to make steam or electricity for sale, claim a feed-in tariff and sell the ash on the side as a fertilizer. For some fuels you can even charge a gate fee instead of paying for them.

Recently there are many more process options. Domestic waste can be processed into RDF – Refuse-Derived Fuel – for sale, and the recycleables (steel, glass, aluminium, etc) recovered for sale. Alternatively you can pyrolyse it to make oil for fuel, or even a feedstuff for plastics manufacture. Forest residue can be compressed into high-value wood fuel pellets, which are growing in popularity; they are now cheaper than gas to heat your house with.

All these are commercial reality. Many of the processes are proven and can be purchased easily – but many more are in development and will hit the market in the next couple of years. All are capable of delivering a profit, but there is one common challenge amongst all these disparate processes, which practical experience has shown us is very often where the profits get lost. This is in the handling and flow of the biomass material into and through the process, which always seems to be given far less consideration than the actual conversion process, even though in reality it often brings as big, or even bigger, challenges.

A typical biomass process plant is shown below.

FIGURE 5.5.1   A typical biomass process plant

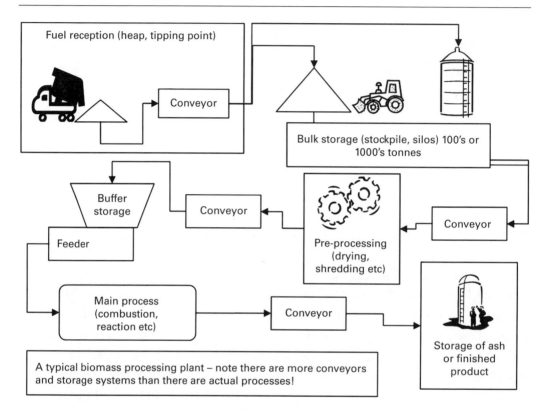

Fuel reception (heap, tipping point)

Conveyor

Bulk storage (stockpile, silos) 100's or 1000's tonnes

Buffer storage

Conveyor

Conveyor

Feeder

Pre-processing (drying, shredding etc)

Main process (combustion, reaction etc)

Conveyor

Storage of ash or finished product

A typical biomass processing plant – note there are more conveyors and storage systems than there are actual processes!

Getting reliable flow of bulk solids is a trickier business than most plant constructors give it credit for – 60 per cent of novel solids processing plants don't reach full capacity even two years after start-up, and cost on average over twice the money budgeted in the business case for construction[1] – but biomass can be amongst the worst.

What is it about biomass?

Industry has handled solid fuel for years. The coal-fired power station has been with us well over a century, and engineers have got the measure of the efficient handling of coal. But the introduction of biomass handled in large quantities has led to major losses and station down-time due to fuel handling system problems.

Examples of common handling problems with biomass

Here are a few of the most common problems that The Wolfson Centre has been asked to troubleshoot in biomass handling:

- poor discharge from silos or hoppers ('arching' or 'rat-holing');
- irregular or inconsistent feeding;
- dust evolution, and biohazards from this ('farmer's lung');
- breakdown of pellets in handling;
- caking (hardening) of materials in storage, from fermentation or mould formation;
- ash heating and hardening following conditioning with water.

All these, and many more common problems, lead to unplanned shutdowns and often expensive plant modifications, seriously denting the marginal profitability of biomass processing and utilization.

Why the problems?

Research at The Wolfson Centre has started to throw light on why many biomass materials are so troublesome for flow. It is often because of the particle shapes. Whereas coal and other 'ordinary' bulk solids tend to have particles which are roughly spherical or block-shaped, often with irregularities, many biomass materials are long and thin (chopped straw or miscanthus), or flat and leafy (shredded sheet material like paper, plastic and card). When they are subjected to stress from a weight of material above, they 'knit' or 'mat' together which makes them hard to move. Many have a low density, so gravity exerts only a small force on them to make them flow. Many are susceptible to biological attack leading to heating and mould formation.

Even after burning, the ash from biomass material behaves quite differently from the ash from coal combustion, so ash handling systems developed from the coal tradition do not work with biomass ashes.

Choosing the right solutions

There are plenty of solutions available for moving, conveying and feeding biomass materials; there is at least one machine option that works for every material. However, many of these machines only work with a narrow range of materials, and it is hard to be sure you choose the right option. Those with the ability to handle the widest range of materials are much more expensive, and may make the project uneconomic. From this it will become obvious that to make a system that is reliable yet affordable, requires a careful choice of the right equipment.

Furthermore, experience shows that the equipment manufacturers are not always as well informed as the buyer expects them to be, when it comes to advising on the right 'tools for the job'. They may be experts in equipment design and manufacture, but you can't really expect them to know about the way in which every possible material they might meet, will behave – *it is up to the buyer* to make sure he selects suitable solutions.

Feedstock variability

Many biomass streams are effectively 'waste' materials. They are often not made to a close specification, and vary from day to day in particle size, dust content, water content etc, much more than most bulk materials. Many are seasonal, so their properties vary – and so do their prices, so it may be desirable to use different feedstocks at different times of year.

Longer term variation in price and availability are an issue. If all the wood-pellet-fired generation stations currently in planning in the UK are built, demand for pellets will outstrip supply by a factor of three; pellet prices will go sky-high, and these facilities will have to burn other feedstocks, for which their fuel handling systems are not designed!

Know your enemy

The messages are:

- All biomass materials handle differently; many are inherently variable.

- Most conveying, feeding and handling systems can cope only with a restricted range of materials; those with wider capability are more expensive!

- Often, facilities designed around one feedstock will have to change to another to maintain profitability.

- It is up to the buyer, not the equipment supplier, to make sure he chooses the right equipment for the materials he is to handle.

Few systems that handle biomass start up and run correctly straight away – many need an extended period of development during which retrofit and lost opportunity costs are incurred, sometimes for a year or two before they get to full operation.

To give yourself a better chance of success:

- Assess, before embarking on a development, what the feedstock is likely to be – not just now, but in the future. Consider the influence of other developments on availability and price.

- Recognize the importance of ensuring the feedstock will flow reliably between reception and process. Don't make the mistake of spending all the time and effort on the conversion (combustion/pyrolysis etc) and leave the material handling to the engineering contractor.

- Above all – *get the feedstock characterized for flow*, not just the favoured material but a range of other options too. This will identify handling equipment that will work from the outset.

- Ensure the contractor takes account of flow property characterization in the equipment they buy, because experience shows they often buy more on price than on technical suitability!

- Before changing the feedstock, get the proposed new material characterized, to see if will go through the handling system you have bought – if not, it's probably best to look elsewhere for suitable feedstock instead of persevering trying to put a 'round peg in a square hole'.

FIGURE 5.5.2   Biomass feedstock

Biomass feedstock – it's cheap and looks innocuous, but can cost you dearly if you don't understand how it is going to behave in your plant

The good news? Recent research has started to deliver meaningful characterization techniques, and these are available to industry. Technical papers from The Wolfson Centre (**www.bulksolids.com**) and the Materials Handling Engineers Association **www.mhea.co.uk** are especially valuable sources of information and should be consulted for further details.

Mike Bradley is the Director of The Wolfson Centre for Bulk Solids Handling Technology, the UK's leading centre for research and independent consultancy in materials handling. His team at The University of Greenwich specializes in all aspects of storage, handling, conveying and processing of loose bulk materials, and provide troubleshooting, system design and product development services to the industry around the globe.

Further details: e-mail: **m.s.a.bradley@gre.ac.uk**.

Note

1 Merrick, E (1990) *Understanding Cost Growth and Performance Shortfall in Novel Process Plants*, The Rand Corporation.

PART SIX
Environment

Water

Cees Buisman and **Leon Korving** at Wetsus review the challenges in developing sustainable technologies in water.

Access to water of the right quality in the right amount is crucial for society to ensure good health and enable economic growth. Given the rising world population and increasing economic growth it is foreseen that within 20 years, there will be a 40 per cent deficit between water demand and available fresh water supplies. It is clear that new water sources must be developed to fill this deficit.

This water issue is not only a water scarcity problem. Increasing use of water also leads to increasing flows of wastewater. If not properly treated, discharge of the wastewater will lead to extensive damage to the environment, including the water sources used for water supply. Treatment for nutrients solely will not be sufficient to secure the quality of water sources. An increasing world population will also imply more use of pharmaceuticals that can accumulate in our environment.

A further complicating factor is that the water issue is closely linked to two other great societal issues: energy supply and food production. Viable solutions for water scarcity and pollution can be developed only in close interaction with the issues of energy and food.

Water is an important production factor for food production, both for agricultural production but also food processing. Overcoming the water deficit is crucial for ensuring sufficient food for the world. As agriculture and the food industry are major water users, it is important to develop solutions in close collaboration with this sector. An important issue is the need for nutrient-rich fertilizers necessary for productive agriculture. Wastewater is an attractive source of nutrients; reuse of these nutrients would save energy needed for fertilizer production and stress on limited resources like phosphate rock.

Just like for water (fuelled by the same trends of population and economic growth), it is expected that there will be an energy deficit. At the same time the use of energy also leads to unwanted emissions damaging the environment, especially the climate. Not only does the fossil energy-based energy sector need a lot of water (eg cooling water) but also the renewable energy sector can be very water-intensive (eg biofuel production). The energy deficit also places a constraint on solutions for water scarcity and pollution, such that only energy-efficient solutions are viable for the future. Most state-of-the-art technologies used to alleviate water scarcity, like desalination, are highly energy-intensive.

Society is thus facing challenges in the field of water, energy and food that are strongly entwined. This situation is referred to as the *water-energy-food nexus*.

At Wetsus we work on the breakthrough solutions that are needed to prepare for this challenge. Our vision is that these challenges can only be solved by a multi-disciplinary approach where people with different skills, knowledge and background work together. This work should take place in close cooperation with private and public stakeholders in an innovation ecosystem where new ideas can be tested and scaled up to real-life applications as fast as possible. At Wetsus we develop new technologies with more than 90 companies and 19 universities. We also provide demonstration sites with partners in our network so new ideas can be tested in real life conditions as soon as possible.

Based on our experience and research in water technology we will give some examples of challenges and solutions that we are developing. We feel the following subjects are of special relevance:

- energy from water;
- control of antibiotic resistance and micro-pollutants;
- nutrient control and recovery.

Energy from water

Energy from water is usually associated with hydropower: that is conversion of water-flow into electricity, be that through a hydroelectric dam or through the conversion of energy from tides or waves. These processes are relatively well-known even if implementation of tidal and wave energy is still in development. Also, increasingly heat from water is being recovered by means of heat pump systems and seasonal thermal energy storage in water aquifers.

Most innovation has to be expected from the conversion of organic matter and salt gradients. Public or industrial wastewater containing organic matter can be used to generate energy. The production of methane from organic matter is a well-studied process but that is more difficult for dilute streams. Bio-electrochemical systems (BES) are innovative processes able to convert the chemical energy present in organic matter directly into electricity. For this, micro-organisms are used as catalysts that will feed on the organic matter and that are able to generate electricity that can be harvested. These systems were long-believed to be a viable solution for energy generation but the trend in this field is going more towards energy-efficient processes. For instance, the European project ValuefromUrine aims to treat urine with such a system, leading to clean water and to the recovery of valuable compounds (mostly phosphorus and nitrogen). While such systems can generate energy of their own, the real added value is the energy that can be saved. The treatment of nitrogen through conventional wastewater treatments is very energy-intensive as it requires the aeration of huge volumes of water. Separately treating the urine, ie the main source of nitrogen in wastewater, with a BES would lead to very significant savings in term of energy required for treating the water.

Salt gradients are also a new source of energy increasingly considered for practical applications. The so-called energy of mixing is the energy lost when two bodies of water of different salinity are mixed. Typically, when river water is mixed with sea water energy is dissipated. As much as 2MJ of energy can be harvested when 1 cubic metre of river water is mixed with a large amount of sea water. Based on the global discharge of river water and seawater, a potential power of approximately 2 TW is available. This is close to the current global electricity consumption. Compared to other ocean energy technologies, salinity gradient energy has the largest energy density. Moreover it has, together with wave and thermal energy, the largest global potential. A large advantage of this form of ocean energy is that harvesting can take place on shore and close to the end-user, since half of the total population lives in coastal areas. Therefore, it holds great promise to become an economical and environmental benign energy resource, available throughout large parts of the world.

Different technologies are being designed to harvest this energy. Reversed electro-dialysis (RED) is a potentially very attractive technology for the production of energy from the mixing of fresh and salt water. In RED, a concentrated salt solution and a less-concentrated salt solution are brought into contact through an alternating series of anion exchange membranes (AEM) and cation exchange membranes (CEM). The membranes separate the concentrated solution from the diluted solution and only ions can pass through the ion selective membranes. Anion exchange membranes contain fixed positive charges which allow anions to permeate through the AEM towards the anode and cation exchange membranes contain fixed negative charges which allow cations to be transported through the CEM towards the cathode. The difference in chemical potential between both solutions is the driving force for this process. At the electrodes a redox (reduction-oxidation) couple is used to mitigate the transfer of electrons.

Figure 6.1.1 shows a schematic representation of the RED technology. Fresh water and sea water exchange ions via ion selective membranes, either cation exchange (C) or anion exchange (A) membranes. At the ends of the membrane piles, electrodes convert the energy into electrical current.

This technology was initially developed at Wetsus and is now further commercialized by Redstack, a spin-off company of Wetsus. Currently Redstack has created a pilot plant facility where scaled-up units can be tested. This pilot plant is located in the North of the Netherlands and aims at a 50-kilowatt (kW) unit.

This same principle is applied in a new idea that is being developed by Wetsus to produce electricity from waste flue gases from (biomass-fired) power plants. Also when releasing flue gas in air the mixing entropy of the systems goes up and thus useful energy has been lost. Mixing flue gas with an excess amount of air gives a much higher energy potential than mixing sweet and salt water, namely 90 MJ/tonne of flue gas. This high-energy density makes flue gas an interesting source for harvesting energy from mixing entropy. This source could potentially produce 967 TWhr per year from power plants, an increase in energy efficiency of 7 per cent. This would reduce the CO_2 emission with 927 million tonnes of CO_2 per year and has an economic value of more than 50 billion euros per year. These are stunning numbers and only making a small part available would be an already valuable achievement.

FIGURE 6.1.1 Schematic representation of the RED technology

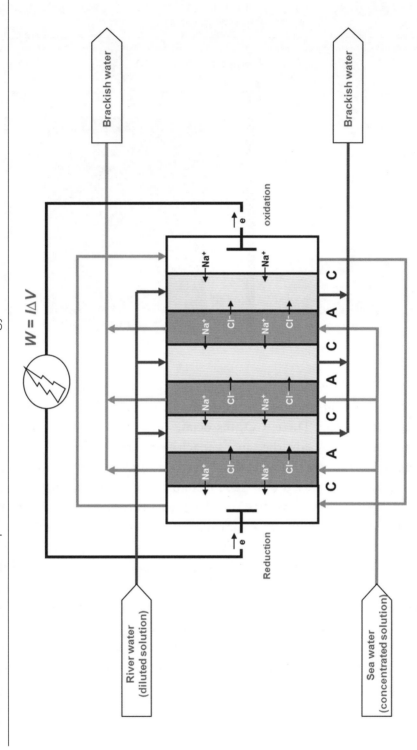

FIGURE 6.1.2   Outline of the CO_2-technology for electricity generation from combustion off-gas

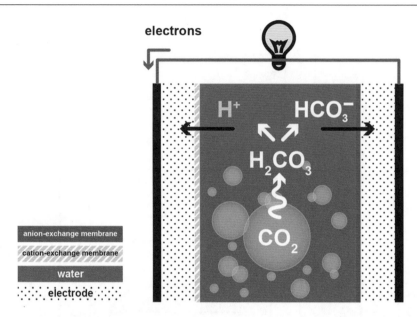

Figure 6.1.2 shows an outline of the CO_2-technology for electricity generation from combustion off-gas. Only the first step is depicted where CO_2 is adsorbed in water. There, CO_2 dissociates in protons and bicarbonate ions that are selectively adsorbed in a capacitive material. This selective adsorption leads to the establishment of an electrical current between the electrodes.

The main challenge for all these technologies is to reach commercial relevance and become competitive with other energy sources. For this, the overall performances of the technologies have to be improved (in terms of gross power production and scale of the installations) and the cost of these technologies has to be decreased. This will happen by optimizing the processes and by selecting materials, very often selective membranes, which are cost-effective. This requires a high implication of the different actors going from researchers that will allow a better understanding of these systems, industries that will help the development of new materials and processes that can be produced on a large scale, and policy makers that can set the appropriate environment for financial and legal support.

Control of antibiotic resistance and pharmaceuticals

An increasing, developing and last but not least aging world population implies an increase of the use of pharmaceuticals in our society. The intensive use of pharmaceuticals has already resulted in polluted water and soil environment. Constant discharge of these compounds happens through different routes, the most important being wastewater. Current wastewater treatment systems are not designed to deal with pharmaceuticals and hormones and the elimination is insufficient. As a result, a slow but certain accumulation is occurring in the environment. For instance, populations of fish have been affected by the exposure to hormones from the birth control pill via wastewater treatment plants.

A more concerning group of pollutants are antibiotics and their metabolites. The use of antibiotics has not only enabled us to treat and prevent all sorts of infections but it has allowed us to produce food efficiently. Unfortunately, the extensive use of antibiotics has led to the development of antibiotic-resistant bacteria. The once very promising and powerful antibiotics are becoming more and more ineffective. Even concentrations below inhibitory levels (like the levels currently found in some wastewaters and sludge) can trigger the development of antibiotic resistance by the transfer of genetic elements from different types of bacteria (human, animal, environmental). This so-called cross-resistance can pose serious consequences to human health. There is evidence that wastewater treatment facilities provide favourable conditions for the spreading of antibiotic resistance into the environment.

The challenge for water technology lies in the development of effective treatment strategies to remove pharmaceuticals, antibiotics and antibiotic resistant genetic elements from wastewater. Considering the societal challenges these strategies should be cost-effective and consume as little energy as possible.

Circa 80 per cent of all human antibiotics are used outside the hospital, but the hospitals use a special class of antibiotics that is our last line of defence against bacterial infections. To prevent resistance to these antibiotics, disinfection at the point of origin of antibiotic resistance is therefore recommended, rather than transport to a central facility where antibiotic resistance can be spread out. Specific wastewater treatment at hospitals can contribute to the containment of bacteria resistance to last-resort antibiotics, preventing high risk to human health.

Within the framework of Denewa, Interreg IV-A project, a demonstration site is being built at the Antonius hospital in Sneek in The Netherlands for the testing of innovative technologies for the treatment of hospital wastewater. In June 2014, different wastewater streams will be available for testing at the demo-site: urine, toilet discharges and combined wastewater. Several partners within the Denewa consortium will test their technologies at this demosite. Among the technologies tested at pilot scale is a technology developed at Wetsus that uses a reactor with numerous TiO_2-coated fluidized UV-LED lights that are powered from the outside of the reactor by induction.

FIGURE 6.1.3   Fluidized UV LEDs with a TiO2 coating

The fluidized UV LEDs with a TiO_2 coating shown in Figure 6.1.3 can be a new energy efficient approach to oxidize micro pollutants in turbid waters.

Nutrient control and recovery

In the last decades sewage water treatment plants have focused on removal of the nutrients nitrogen and phosphorus from wastewater and this strategy has been very successful in preventing eutrophication of surface waters.

However the challenges ahead require us to rethink these technologies so that they not only become more energy-efficient but also make it possible to recycle valuable nutrients. This can provide new opportunities to create value from wastewater, thus creating new business models for the treatment of sewage.

Management of nitrogen is mainly an energy issue: it requires a lot of energy (37 kJ/g N) to produce nitrogen fertilizers from air. These fertilizers are then used to grow crops that are used as food for humans or feed for livestock. After consumption the nitrogen ends up in sewage or manure. In sewage treatment plants nitrification and de-nitrification processes are used to convert the nitrogen back to nitrogen gas. This is also an energy intensive process that even requires as much energy (45 kJ/g N) as the production of nitrogen fertilizers. Already de-ammonification processes have been developed that can reduce the energy consumption for nitrogen removal (16 kJ/g N), but until now these processes are limited to warm (> 30°C) wastewater streams like sludge dewatering liquors. Pilot plant testing is now carried out at two locations (Nieuwveer: UNAS, Dokhaven: CINERELTA) in The Netherlands to advance the application of this technology to colder wastewater (5–15°C). This would open the way for de-ammonification in the main water line of a sewage water treatment plant. This will in turn provide another benefit for energy recovery from wastewater as de-ammonification does not require a carbon source for nitrogen removal. Therefore the soluble COD can now be removed from the wastewater by transformation into sewage sludge in a high loaded biological system. The produced sludge can be digested to generate biogas.

The bio-electrochemical systems that were described earlier can further increase the energy-efficiency of nitrogen management. Research at Wetsus (ValuefromUrine) shows that these systems can recover ammonia from urine without using external energy. The ammonia can be reused as a fertilizer, thus saving the energy requirement to produce nitrogen fertilizer from air.

Management of phosphorous presents very different challenges. Unlike nitrogen, phosphorus cannot be released in the atmosphere and has to be concentrated in a waste stream, normally sewage sludge. This creates a waste problem that presents significant costs for operators of sewage water-treatment plants. In a large part of the world the sewage sludge is used as a biosolid in agriculture. For rural areas this can be a very effective use of the sludge, but can be more problematic for densely populated and industrialized areas. In these areas the load of nutrients in the sludge exceeds the nutrient demand in the areas that are at a reasonable transport distance from the cities. In addition the sewage is often polluted with heavy metals and micro-pollutants so that this practice may lead to public resistance.

On the other hand, resources of phosphate rock are not abundantly available: three countries in the world are responsible for 70 per cent of the world production of phosphate rock: China (39 per cent), the United States (16 per cent) and Morocco/Western Sahara (15 per cent). Both the United States and China have a very large domestic consumption and hardly export phosphate rock. Therefore Middle Eastern and North African countries dominate the world market of phosphate rock. The remaining lifetime of the world reserves is the subject of debate and estimates vary between 100 to 300 years. The large concentration of phosphate rock reserves in a small number of countries is probably more important for the availability and price of phosphate rock than the size of the reserves. This was illustrated in 2008 when prices for phosphate rock peaked at US $350 per tonne when they had been for decade US $40 to US $50 per tonne. After the global financial crisis in 2008 prices came down, but levelled off at US $150 to US $200 per tonne, still much higher than before.

Recovery of phosphorus from wastewater can therefore contribute to food security by offering alternative sources of phosphate. At the same time it reduces waste production and costs for waste handling. The challenge for phosphorus recovery is to produce products from sewage that have a high added value so that they can be transported from areas where there is a surplus of phosphorus (urbanized areas) to areas where there is demand (rural areas). In addition these products should be free of contaminants in order to protect the environment and maintain the quality of our surface water.

Already technologies are available for recovery of phosphorus from wastewater. One interesting development is the recovery of phosphorus from sewage sludge ashes. Existing wet chemical processes for processing of low-grade phosphate rock can be modified to use this as an alternative raw material. In The Netherlands two large sewage sludge incinerators process 50 per cent of all sewage sludge from the country and can therefore provide significant volumes of ash. Plans for the realization of a full-scale treatment facility are reaching their final stage and it is expected that full-scale processing can start in 2016.

However not all countries can or want to invest in costly sewage sludge incinerators and therefore alternatives for recovery of phosphorus in the sewage treatment plant are required. Crystallization of struvite (magnesium ammonium phosphate) is an interesting approach to recover phosphorus in a relatively pure and concentrated form from wastewater. It requires high concentrations of soluble phosphate and these can only be found in sewage-treatment plants that apply enhanced biological phosphorus removal in combination with sludge digestion. Unfortunately most operators rely on iron-based chemicals to remove phosphate from sewage water. No viable method is yet available to recover phosphorus in a pure form from these types of sewage water-treatment plants. Wetsus is therefore researching methods that can be applied in these plants.

Conclusion

The developments in our society present a large number of challenges for water technology. A coordinated and multidisciplinary approach is essential to provide radical solutions for the next generations. At Wetsus we are building a research network with strong interactions with private and public stakeholders so that we can provide an ecosystem where these solutions can mature quickly so they can contribute to society as fast as possible.

The Wetsus Centre of Excellence for Sustainable Water Technology is a facilitating intermediary for trend-setting scientific knowhow development. Wetsus creates a unique environment and strategic cooperation for development of profitable and sustainable state-of-the-art water treatment technology. The inspiring and multidisciplinary collaboration between more than 90 global companies and 19 European universities in Wetsus results in innovations that contribute significantly to the solution of the global water problems. Within Wetsus research clusters of about eight companies are started on a high-commitment high-trust basis with a focus to investigate breakthrough ideas and scale them up. Wetsus is co-funded by the Dutch Ministry of Economic Affairs and Ministry of Infrastructure and Environment, the European Regional Development Fund, the Province of Fryslân, and the Northern Netherlands

Further details: website: **http://wetsus.nl.**

WaterCampus Leeuwarden wants to function as the European hub for water technology. The wide variety of organizations based at the WaterCampus creates an inspiring environment, offering opportunities to exchange knowledge and skills. The WaterCampus is a joint development of Wetsus, Water Alliance, Centre of Expertise Water Technology (CEW), Centre of Innovative Craftmanship Water (CIV Water), Water Application Centre (WAC), Municipality Leeuwarden and the Fryslân Province. At WaterCampus we combine science and education with research and entrepreneurship.

Further information is available from Wetsus, Centre of Excellence for Sustainable Water Technology, Oostergoweg 7, 8911 MA Leeuwarden, The Netherlands (e-mail: **leon.korving@wetsus.nl**).

Current priorities for air pollution control

Professor Duncan Laxen, Managing Director of Air Quality Consultants Ltd, sets out the current priorities for tackling air pollution in the UK.

W e have come a long way in tackling air pollution over the last few decades. Airborne lead pollution is now a thing of the past, thanks to legislation requiring unleaded petrol, carbon monoxide and benzene concentrations at the roadside are now a fraction of what they used to be, thanks to the introduction of catalytic converters and sulphur dioxide concentrations are also well down, thanks to the use of low sulphur fuels and flue gas desulphurization in power stations.

But all is still not well. The government has estimated that around 29,000 deaths a year can be attributed to air pollution, and the UK Government is being threatened with court proceedings for failure to meet the European Union (EU) limit values. The deaths are attributable to exposure to fine airborne particles, while the court proceedings are due to high levels of nitrogen dioxide.

The key pollutants today are fine airborne particles, which are measured as particulate matter (PM) with an aerodynamic diameter of 2.5 or 10 micrometres ($PM_{2.5}$ and PM_{10}), and nitrogen dioxide; and it is these pollutants that are largely driving policy initiatives. Ozone is also a pollutant that causes health impacts and damage to crops and ecosystems, but it is a regional pollutant and, as such, seems to receive less attention. Fine airborne particles penetrate deep into the lung. It is believed that some of these particles are small enough to pass through into the blood stream, and that this is one of the ways that exposure can lead to health impacts. The 29,000 deaths a year that can be attributed to exposure to PM are mainly for heart disease, followed by respiratory conditions and then cancer. There is no evidence for a safe level of exposure to PM.

Nitrogen dioxide is an irritant gas that can aggravate conditions for asthmatics. Its role in contributing to deaths is less clear and it is generally treated as being less harmful than PM. One reason for this uncertainty is that concentrations of PM and nitrogen dioxide are highly correlated in the atmosphere, and it is difficult to disentangle the separate effects that these two pollutants are having. There is, though, growing evidence that nitrogen dioxide is having its own effect on health, and it is not just an indicator for effects from PM. When it comes to setting standards, nitrogen dioxide has been treated as being a pollutant with a threshold below which effects are insignificant. This is not the case for PM and every microgramme per cubic metre ($\mu g/m^3$) reduction in exposure has essentially the same beneficial effect, whatever the concentration. It is for this reason that a new approach has been developed for $PM_{2.5}$, whereby an overall reduction in exposure is required over a 10-year period. The target for the UK is a 15 per cent reduction over the 10 years between 2010 and 2020.

Particulate matter is strictly not 'a' pollutant, as it represents a wide range of chemicals that form particles of a wide variety of sizes and shapes, in some cases 'coating' other particles; the composition of PM changes from place to place and with time of day and time of year. We are currently in the position where all particles have to be treated as having the same toxicity, so the aim must be to reduce exposure to all PM, irrespective of source. Nitrogen dioxide is more straightforward, but not completely so, as it is formed and removed from the air by chemical reactions. We therefore focus on the emissions of nitrogen oxides, as it is these emissions that determine the concentrations of nitrogen dioxide. The term 'nitrogen oxides' refers essentially to two gases: nitric oxide and nitrogen dioxide. Nitrogen oxides are generated during combustion and consist mainly of nitric oxide. Once in the atmosphere the nitric oxide is converted to nitrogen dioxide by reacting with ozone (this is why ozone concentrations are low close to fresh emissions of nitrogen oxides). During daylight hours, sunlight can destroy nitrogen dioxide, converting it back to nitric oxide, adding to the complexity of nitrogen dioxide concentrations.

Airborne PM arises from many different sources, and this makes it particularly difficult to manage exposure. It is emitted as particles from combustion processes and arises from dust raised from a wide range of sources, some of which are natural. The natural particles include sea salt. These particles are all called *primary* PM. In addition, particles are formed in the atmosphere from gases, some of which are also natural in origin, although most are due to human activity. These are *secondary* particles, and they tend to be formed hundreds of kilometres downwind of the source of the precursor gas emissions. Primary particles affect concentrations mostly close to the source and are local in scale, while secondary particles give rise to elevated concentrations over a wider area and are regional in scale. Primary PM emissions are more straightforward to build into a control strategy, as a reduction in local emissions will lead to a reduction in concentrations of primary PM. Secondary PM on the other hand is less straightforward to manage, as the precursor gas emissions can be many kilometres away, and the chemistry involved in their formation means that a 30 per cent reduction in precursor gas emissions, for example of sulphur dioxide, may only lead to a 15 per cent reduction in secondary PM; the chemistry makes the relationship non-linear. Unfortunately secondary PM accounts for around half the $PM_{2.5}$ concentrations found in urban areas.

Control of $PM_{2.5}$ concentrations will clearly require emissions from a wide range of sources to be controlled. The primary PM controls will need to cover vehicle exhaust, brake- and tyre-wear, biomass combustion, waste handling, industrial activities and construction activities. Secondary PM will require controls across Europe on emissions of sulphur dioxide, largely from power stations and shipping, nitrogen oxides, from power stations and motor vehicles, and ammonia mainly from agricultural activities; these gases being the precursor emissions of ammonium sulphate and ammonium nitrate that dominate secondary PM.

High nitrogen dioxide concentrations largely arise from emissions of nitrogen oxides from motor vehicles, and the highest concentrations are thus found alongside busy streets. Concentrations fall off rapidly on moving away from the road and the majority of exceedances of the air quality objectives for nitrogen dioxide are at residential properties that lie within a few metres of the kerb. These exceedances are widespread, and even occur in relatively small towns. In London, the exceedances can even occur away from the roads, due to the general build-up of pollution levels in the centre of the city. Back in 2000, we thought that the stringent new regulations on emissions from motor vehicles would have eliminated all exceedances by now, but this has not come to pass. Indeed concentrations have hardly fallen at all over the last 13 years. This is because the new regulations on motor vehicle emissions have not delivered what was promised. This is especially the case for diesel vehicles – cars, vans, lorries and buses. Somehow the motor vehicle manufacturers have ensured that the vehicles pass the test, but when the vehicles are driven on the road, the emissions are not any lower than those of vehicles built to previous less stringent standards. Smaller sources, such as combined heat and power (CHP) plant, can also be significant local sources, as they can worsen an existing exceedance, and their emissions also need to be considered.

Nitrogen oxides emissions are not just an urban problem. They can increase the amount of nitrogen being deposited to sensitive ecosystems. Special areas of conservation (SACs) have been designated across the UK and they have a high level of protection. As consultants, we are increasingly being asked to address the impacts of new developments, such as anaerobic digestion plants, on these SACs. It is important therefore that nitrogen oxides emissions are reduced wherever they occur. This requires the motor vehicle manufacturers and regulators to deliver real reductions in emissions from new vehicles. It also requires reductions in nitrogen oxides emissions from point sources. These reductions will reduce exposure to high nitrogen dioxide concentrations, as well as reduce nitrogen deposition to sensitive ecosystems. In addition, they will reduce high summer-time ozone concentrations and secondary $PM_{2.5}$ concentrations, as nitrogen oxides emissions play a part in both of these.

There is clearly still much to do to tackle air pollution in the UK. The remaining pollutants, $PM_{2.5}$, nitrogen dioxide and ozone are all particularly challenging. They all depend on chemical reactions taking place in the atmosphere, so are not related in a simple way to emissions, as was the case in the past with sulphur dioxide from coal burning and lead from the use of leaded petrol. They are all to a greater or lesser extent regional pollutants. The harmful effects these pollutants are causing still justify strenuous actions to reduce emissions, and many will have to play a part in delivering this, from developers to members of the public, and from politicians to regulators.

Professor Duncan Laxen is Managing Director of Air Quality Consultants Ltd. He is a visiting Professor in Air Quality Management and Assessment at the University of the West of England, Bristol and a Fellow of the Institute of Air Quality Management. He has been a member of a number of government expert groups, including the Air Quality Expert Group and the Committee on the Medical Effects of Air Pollutants. His company has just celebrated its 20-year anniversary, and with 16 staff it is one of the largest air quality consultancy groups in the UK. The company provides expert advice and assessment on a wide range of air quality issues across the UK and abroad.

Further details: e-mail: **DuncanLaxen@aqconsultants.co.uk**; website: **www.aqconsultants.co.uk**.

Resource efficiency

To cut waste, become a circular thinker, says **Katherine Adams** at BRE.

One of the latest buzzwords in the arena of resource efficiency is 'circular economy'. Put simply, this is all about using resources for a long as possible and at the same time extracting the maximum amount of value from them – a move away from the linear economy (make, use and dispose). Related to this are important issues such as the reduction of waste, greater resource productivity (ie producing more with less), reducing our environmental impacts, being more competitive and helping to address emerging resource scarcity/security issues. All of the above make good business sense. This article focuses on the circular economy and how this thinking can be applied practically and the associated benefits that can be made.

The problem

The world's population has passed the 7 billion mark and the UN estimates suggest that this could rise to nearly 11 billion by 2050. Several recent studies show that Earth's resources are enough to sustain only about 2 billion people at a European standard of living. The future of our resources is therefore critical, and this is where circular economy thinking is embedded.

Approximately 540 million tonnes of resources (direct material) were used in the UK in 2010 and 249 million tonnes of waste was generated; of this 117 million tonnes was recycled (ie kept within the material loop). This shows that are still large savings to be made in:

- reducing the amount of materials used by being smarter with our designs or material choice;

- reducing the amount of waste produced;
- reusing and/or recycling more waste.

Nearly a third of profit warnings issued by FTSE 350 companies in 2011 were attributed to rising resource prices, suggesting that there is a significant relationship between resource efficiency and competitiveness.

The opportunity

Most of the value in the circular economy comes much higher up the chain (or loop). Recycling is, in fact, a last resort as the major opportunity lies with the remanufacture, refurbishing and reselling of goods. A 2012 report from the Ellen MacArthur Foundation, with analysis by McKinsey, has placed a material cost saving opportunity of adopting the circular opportunity in Europe of between US $340 billion and US $630 billion per annum by 2025.

In terms of waste costs to the end user, the cost of the product far outweighs the cost of disposal and recovery. If you flip this around, there is significant inherent value in the waste stream that is largely untapped. This value includes the material resources, and the time, energy and other resources used in manufacturing and distribution. The largest commercial opportunities therefore revolve around retaining as much of this value as possible, including the resources needed to manufacture and distribute. A number of actions are considered critical in moving to a circular economy. These are outlined below.

Design

How we design our products is critical, in terms of the amount and type of materials that are used, how they are used and how long the products last, and if they can be reused and/or recycled at the end of life. Approximately 80 per cent of a product's environmental impact has already been decided at the design stage. Innovation is key here: How do we ensure we innovate to embrace technology and sustainable thinking? I work in the construction sector, where products have a longer lifespan than other sectors and as such it can be harder to implement change in the short term. An example of this is cars, which are now designed for their components to be disassembled easily and reused/recycled at end of life. For buildings, this is a more complex issue. A typical construction project involves thousands of components and very often little consideration is given to end of life thinking. More products are now being used in buildings, which, with current technology, are hard to recover.

New business models

Many of our business models are based on the 'make sell, use and dispose' philosophy (especially in the construction sector). There is no onus on a manufacturer or seller of a product to have responsibility for the product, unless this is a requirement of legislation. There is therefore little incentive for the manufacturer to design for reuse, remanufacture or longevity. A move towards more leasing of products would help to shift attitudes here. There is also a need to base contracts on the functional performance requirements rather than the product specification itself.

Product collection and reuse

Logistics are important. How can we, in the most efficient way, collect products that are redundant and ensure that they are kept within the same product loop to ensure remanufacture and reuse opportunities? Most examples of this come from the consumer product market, whereby electrical goods can be taken back by the manufacturer or indeed by the seller of the new product, providing an incentive to buy. In construction, there are examples of this, such as the take back by manufacturers of carpet tiles, plasterboard and ceiling tiles.

System changes

To allow a circular economy to flourish, system changes are required. We need a regulatory framework that supports the 'circular economy' and facilitates appropriate industry standards and incentives. For example, in the construction sector, it can be difficult to reuse certain products from a perceived risk and insurance issue.

How can I adopt circular thinking?

This depends on your role. If you are a designer, be it a product, system or building, then perhaps you need to think about your material choice and examine the product at the end of its life (a rarity). Can you disassemble it without any need of specialized equipment? Can it be remanufactured? Can it be reused? Can it be recycled? If your component is being added to another component, then does the fixing aid deconstruction?

If you manufacture as well as design, then can you look at your processes for reducing resource use? Can you collect it at end of life and remanufacture? Can you ensure that you can use the material as a feedstock for your new products? If you sell products, can you look at changing your business model? Will this, in fact, give you an advantage over your competitors? If you buy products, then you need to be asking these sorts of questions of your supply chain. Measurement is also crucial, in understanding resource use and waste generation and where improvements can be made. BRE's SMARTWaste is an online reporting system that can help users in the construction sector identify their key waste streams and look at these improvements.

What does the future hold?

The term 'circular economy' may disappear in the future, but the key components of it are likely to stay, purely from a forward-thinking business perspective. An EU advisory panel is recommending that goods manufactured and sold in Europe have a 'product passport', or a declaration of what materials are used and their potential for reuse at the end of the product's life. To be ahead of the game, you need to be thinking in circles!

Prepared by **Katherine Adams**, Principal Consultant, BRE (tel: 01923 664478; e-mail: **adamsk@bre.co.uk**; website: **www.smartwaste.co.uk**).

BRE is an independent and impartial, research-based consultancy, testing and training organization, offering expertise in every aspect of the built environment and associated industries. We help clients create better, safer and more sustainable products, buildings, communities and businesses – and we support the innovation needed to achieve. BRE is owned by the BRE Trust, which is the largest UK charity dedicated specifically to research and education in the built environment. Further details: website: **www.bre.co.uk**.

PART SEVEN
Transport

OXIS ENERGY

Next Generation Battery Technology

+44 (0)1865 407 017
info@oxisenergy.com
www.oxisenergy.com

IT S SAFER WITH OXIS

REVOLUTIONARY ELECTRIC VEHICLE BATTERY [REVB]

The Project
Revolutionary
Electric Vehicle Battery

The Consortium
OXIS Energy (Lead partner)
Imperial College London
Cranfield University
Lotus Engineering

The Project Targets
400Wh/kg. Half the weight of current
Li-ion EV battery systems

The Final Deliverable
Li-S battery and powertrain,
proven in Lotus EV simulator, delivery 2016

Powering tomorrow's electric vehicles

Dr Mark Crittenden and **Huw Hampson-Jones** at OXIS Energy Ltd discuss the future of electric vehicles.

Has the electric vehicle (EV) uptake gone to plan?

'No' is the quick answer. Go along to any EV conference today, and you'll hear presenters admitting that the uptake figures for EVs predicted a few years ago were overambitious. The key questions to answer are: When will EV adoption take off and replace the conventional Internal Combustion Engine? And: What has held back this enormous growth prediction? Let's start with the latter.

The first key constraint is known as 'Range Anxiety'. This essentially is the concern that a vehicle has insufficient range to reach the desired destination and the occupants of the vehicle will be left stranded. Clearly, anxiety levels will reduce as the vehicle range increases. Without technological improvements, increasing vehicle range requires designing heavier batteries into a vehicle, which impacts manoeuvrability and fuel economy. A lighter technology would allow the range to be increased without negatively impacting the vehicle.

The second key constraint is safety. A series of high-profile accidents continue to undermine confidence in battery technology. The Boeing 787 Dreamliner fleet was grounded by the Federal Aviation Administration in January 2013 for over 3 months, following multiple safety incidents including fires. Tesla has also had fires in their vehicles. How justifiable the press coverage has been, considering the number of Tesla vehicles, is open for debate, but what is undeniable is a loss of confidence in battery safety. Safety can be improved through physically protecting the batteries, but this only adds unwanted weight while reducing range.

For there to be a dramatic change in the number of EVs on our roads, battery technology needs to improve both in terms of reduced weight and safety, whilst ensuring that pricing is competitive. The battery technology available today is not up to the job, but fortunately there are new battery chemistries on the horizon – lithium air has been widely publicized, but most industry analysts agree that this will not be ready until at least 2030. Lithium sulfur is seen therefore by many as the next battery chemistry to fill this gap.

Some history first – the domination of the internal combustion engine

The first demonstration EVs were produced in the 1830s, but were only commercially produced from the late 19th century with the introduction of mass-produced rechargeable batteries. In fact the first car to break the mile-a-minute barrier was Gaston de Chasseloup-Laubat in the Jeantaud Duc EV in 1898. By the 1920s several hundred thousand EVs had been produced. However the internal combustion engine soon began to dominate due to its superior specific energy. Specific energy, measured in Wh/kg (**watt-hours per kilogram**), is the ratio of the energy stored to the mass. Petrol has a specific energy of around 9,000 Wh/kg, compared to lead acid at 30 Wh/kg so, with little consideration to the environmental impact, there was only going to be one winner.

Other technologies have since improved on lead acid, including nickel metal hydride, with Li-ion batteries now being the main EV battery chemistry, achieving over 100 Wh/kg. However Li-ion batteries are beginning to reach their maximum potential so there is increasing interest in new chemistries to push the performance further.

Introducing lithium sulfur

Lithium sulfur (Li-S) is a fundamentally different electrochemistry to Li-ion, which conventionally contains carbon in the anode and lithium in the cathode.

In the case of Li-S, a cell consists of layers of lithium metal anodes protected by a lithium sulfide passivation layer, sulfur-based cathodes, separators and electrolyte. Layers are stacked many times and packaged in an aluminium laminate pouch to construct the complete cell. Upon discharge the sulfur contained within the cathode reacts with lithium ions which release electrons. Since sulfur is an insulating material, carbon is also added to the cathode to enhance the electrical conductivity. Polymer is then used to bind the cathode together.

Safety

Conventional electrochemical wisdom holds that the use of lithium metal is risky. A common belief is that any rechargeable lithium metal system will sooner or later generate uncontrolled dendritic lithium. Fortunately, this is not the case for lithium sulfur: the electrolytes provide an effective mechanism for the passivation of suspended or 'mossy' lithium by creating a lithium sulfide film on the lithium, which protects the metal from abuse.

To use the adage that a system is only as safe as its weakest point, it is also very important to formulate an electrolyte with a high flash point and thus a low flammability. Using a good choice of electrolyte, coupled with the passivation layer, safe operation has been demonstrated up to 85 degrees centigrade, albeit with reduced capacity at the top end of this range, with no safety issues when the cells are heated up to 140 degrees centigrade. Such cells have also been subjected to a barrage of abuse tests including overcharge, short circuit, nail and bullet penetration tests, both on freshly assembled and cycled cells. All of these tests have been passed without any adverse reaction and with no measurable increase in the size of the cells.

Performance

Systems using metallic lithium are known to offer the highest specific energy, and coupled with sulfur, have a theoretical density of over 2700 Wh/kg, 5 times that of Li-ion. 350 Wh/kg has already been demonstrated in coin and small pouch cells and 240 Wh/kg in production-size pouch cells. So for the same energy stored, the battery will be significantly lighter.

The cells have a 100 per cent available depth-of-discharge, compared to Li-ion batteries which are often only used across 80 per cent (or less) of their available discharge range, and are damaged by over-discharge. If a battery cannot be fully discharged, in order to meet the capacity requirement for the maximum discharge scenarios, the battery has to be oversized, increasing weight and cost.

Until recently most of the Li-S research has been directed at increasing specific energy and, as these figures are now very competitive, other aspects are receiving much more attention. Cycle life – the number of times a cell or battery can be charged and discharged – has historically been relatively low but, by choosing better materials, cycle life is now improving dramatically. Such figures are usually quoted as '80 per cent Beginning Of Life', which is when the capacity drops to 80 per cent of the initial capacity. Figures over 1,000 cycles can now be achieved, and figures of 2,000 cycles are looking increasingly realistic.

The cells described have been shown to have a long shelf-life with no charging required to prevent damage when left for extended periods. In comparison, Li-ion batteries require regular recharge to prevent failure and this is often the cause of warranty issues for manufacturers and suppliers.

Clean tech

The Li-S chemistry is considered to have less environmental impact when compared to other technologies such as Li-ion. The Li-S cell utilizes sulfur in place of heavy metals such as nickel and cobalt, having an environmental impact if they enter the food chain in concentrations that would otherwise not occur naturally. Both lithium and sulfur occur naturally: sulfur is found in large concentrations around volcanoes and deposits in the United States; for manufacturing it can be obtained as a recycled by-product from the oil industry. Lithium or its salts are abundant in rocks and spring waters. As the cells have fewer compounds than Li-ion cells, they are expected to be less complex to recycle – this was in fact the subject of a recent project, funded by the Technology Strategy Board, the UK's Innovation Agency, where G and P Batteries and OXIS Energy determined the process to recover lithium from end-of-life cells.

The first lithium sulfur vehicle

The first commercially available vehicle with a Li-S battery will be the Induct Navia. The Navia is a driverless eight-passenger robotized shuttle, designed for transportation in city centres or private campuses such as airport car parks, shopping malls, business parks and universities. It is equipped with laser range finders, cameras and a software package that allows it to move autonomously and safely in any environment. The cells will be mass-produced by GP Batteries who are a major global manufacturer of primary and rechargeable batteries, and the largest consumer battery manufacturer in China. As the homogenization process for the mass car market is generally expected to take about five years, vehicles such as the Navia will help prove the technology to the wider market.

Mass-market adoption

For the successful adoption of EVs into the mass market, the performance of the technology needs to be improved even further whilst ensuring a competitive price. To this end, the Technology Strategy Board is funding the Revolutionary Electric Vehicle Battery project with OXIS Energy, Lotus Engineering, Imperial College London and Cranfield University. This will improve the Li-S battery chemistry and production methods in order to exceed 400 Wh/kg and achieve other key performance parameters. The project is developing simulation-modelling techniques for Li-S in order to speed up research improvements and be used as a basis for real-time control algorithms to allow maximum utilization of energy over a complete system lifetime, without compromising performance.

The output of the project will be to integrate and prove the entire system with a powertrain by the end of 2016. Through these improvements, vehicles should be in production from 2018. To answer our first question, with the key constraints of safety and range anxiety overcome, we predict the EV market to grow strongly from that year.

EV battery improvements benefit other applications

Improvements made in battery technology for the EV market will also have enormous benefits to non-EV applications. Solar energy storage has become a rapidly growing market, the key driver for which is the need to reduce energy bills. Consider a typical household who has installed solar panels on their home. In the daytime, when the family are at work or school, the majority of the energy generated by the panels is sold to the grid at relatively small rates. In the evening, when the family has returned and needs electricity, they have to buy this back from the grid at higher rates. In the UK, the difference between selling and buying is around US $0.11 per kWh, and this figure will only increase as electricity prices rise (in South Africa an annual electricity price increase of 15 to 20 per cent has been predicted for the next five years). Consumers want a cost-effective solution that is safe in their homes and is not a large, heavy installation.

The Defence industry also has a strong desire to reduce costs. In a 2011 study of a US Forward Operating Base, it was found that due to costly transportation, the real cost of diesel at the front line was found to be US $70 per litre; through the use of solar energy, they were able to save US $7,000 per day. Using lightweight and safe batteries in such situations will allow a rapid and safer deployment.

Lightening the load on soldiers is a priority issue for the UK MoD (Ministry of Defence) and with each patrol soldier currently carrying around 8 kilograms in batteries alone, halving this weight would be a significant benefit.

With pollution an increasing problem, particularly around harbours, there is an increasing desire, backed with legislation, to reduce this through the use of electric motors powered by batteries. Safety is paramount at sea and a lightweight battery allows boats to be designed with a greater range. Furthermore as the technology required has much in common with automobiles, development timescales are reduced.

Li-S batteries are now being developed for all these applications. For instance, the Defence Science and Technology Laboratory are funding the development of Li-S batteries for UK forces. Here safety is critical in a hostile environment and this work has even proved that OXIS Li-S cells can survive being punctured by a bullet, not only with no adverse reaction, but with the cells continuing to operate.

Looking further ahead – lithium air

Beyond lithium sulfur, lithium air offers huge potential, combining oxygen from air with lithium, giving a theoretical specific energy of over 11,000 Wh/kg. One of the main research activities here is the IBM Battery 500 project, which started in 2009, with the goal of achieving 500 miles (800 km) range per charge, with a total electric drive system comparable in size, weight and price to a gasoline drive train.

The IBM researchers have successfully demonstrated the fundamental chemistry of the charge-and-recharge process for lithium air batteries. However there are many challenges to overcome – IBM themselves see this as 'a very high-risk/very high-reward, long-horizon project' and many would agree that it will be at least 2030, or even 2040, before the technology will be in practical applications.

It is only with these new chemistries that we will truly see the downfall of the internal combustion engine and a cleaner environment.

Huw Hampson-Jones is the Chief Executive Officer and **Dr Mark Crittenden** the Business Development Manager at OXIS Energy Ltd, Culham Science Centre, Abingdon, Oxfordshire, UK.

Since 2005 OXIS Energy has been at the forefront of developing the innovative Lithium Sulfur technology that is about to revolutionize the rechargeable battery market.

For more information, please contact OXIS Energy (tel: 01865 407017; e-mail: **info@oxisenergy.com**; website: **www.oxisenergy.com**).

Transport design 7.2

Think differently for cleaner solutions, argues **Paul Priestman**
at Priestmangoode.

While I'm a product designer by training, my company, Priestmangoode, has, over the last 15 years, specialized in transport and aviation design. In that time, the industry has changed enormously, not least due to rising environmental concerns over carbon emissions. Personally, my philosophy has always been to try and make things better and more efficient, to build, run and maintain. But in recent years the need for sustainability, in the truest sense of the word, has become palpable. Attitudes within the transport industry have changed, as has consumer behaviour. This, along with fast-developing technology, means that today is a particularly exciting time to be working in transport.

Environmental issues aside, younger generations and the change in consumer behaviour they have engendered, are at the heart of clean tech in transport. Individual car ownership was something to aspire to for previous generations, while increasingly consumers prefer car sharing and collaborative consumption. 'Peak car' – the hypothesis that motor vehicle distance travelled per person by private car has peaked and will continue to fall in a sustained manner – is a truth widely accepted today as far as urban transport is concerned. As more and more people live in cities, fewer need private cars and are looking for other, more sustainable and more economical modes of transport.

This shift in behaviour is readily perceivable in transport design and in particular, in design education. In 2013, I was asked to captain a jury team for an international transport design award. Out of countless entries – both from students and professional designers – not a single one was for a private vehicle. We saw bicycles made of bamboo, agricultural vehicles designed for dual use as public transport in rural India and sharing schemes to reduce private vehicle usage in city centres. It's encouraging to see that both supply and demand are leading us towards mass transit and collaborative consumption.

One recent development is the emergence of driverless technology in the public realm. At the end of 2013, the government announced a £1.5 million project to design and construct the first driverless vehicles to run in a UK city centre. Twenty autonomous pods will take passengers from Milton Keynes train station to the city centre. While I applaud the investment in the research and development of the technology, we need to apply it to mass transit, solutions that will benefit many, not just a few. That is where the future of transport lies.

I have always been a vocal supporter of public transport, and high-speed rail in particular. In 2013, I was appointed Global Creative Director of CSR Sifang, one of the world's largest rolling stock manufacturers. My company has been working with them for the last few years designing high-speed trains in China and the rest of the world. Being so involved in infrastructure projects all around the world has shown me the importance of investment in large infrastructure projects as crucial to a greener future. But as vast amounts of money are invested, we must think about clean tech investment into all areas surrounding transport, not just the vehicles themselves. I'm astounded that the technology of rolling stock vehicles today has evolved so much, yet these high-technology trains are running on a system that was designed over two centuries ago.

Clean technology isn't just about developing new products and services, it's about applying a different kind of thinking to find solutions to everyday problems that will benefit our environment as well as passengers. Designers are trained to think differently and the UK has an extraordinary wealth of design talent, from employing some of the best designers in the world to a design education that is equal to none. We must harness this strength and keep it at the heart of the growth of clean tech industries.

My company works predominantly in public transport, so whatever we design needs to last for the next 50 years. It's led us to think differently about things, to not accept the status quo and to constantly challenge the norm. Having worked on so many high-speed rail projects around the world for instance, I'm adamant that there are better, more efficient, greener ways of running these new high-technology trains, than by having them stop at stations. As a result, my company developed the Moving Platforms concept, a completely inter-connected rail infrastructure where local trams connect to a network of non-stop high speed trains enabling passengers to travel from their local stop to a local address at their destination (even in another country) without getting off a train. The totally joined-up network would allow passengers to transfer directly from one moving tram or high-speed train to another. This new infrastructure mimics the way the internet works, creating a system similar to the one that allows your home PC to connect to a computer on the other side of the world via a series of connected networks.

FIGURE 7.2.1   Priestmangoode's *Moving Platforms* concept

All around the world, new 21st-century train services are being built on a station-based infrastructure that was designed in the 19th century for steam trains. We should be re-thinking infrastructure and building an inter-connected local-to-global rail network. Current plans for high-speed rail will require a new network of major stations, taking up huge amounts of space and with a cost and environmental impact that is potentially vast. These stations function for the most part as large car parks that are packed during working hours and empty the rest of the time, and are only in use by passengers for short periods of the day.

In addition, a major problem with high-speed trains is that they are not very fast. Slowing down and speeding up as they move between stations means they are only able to travel at their full speed for limited periods of time (wasting vast amounts of energy in the process). Many rail passengers use cars to get to their main-line embarkation station, so being able to link up to the high speed train directly from a local tram or train service means we could reduce car usage in towns and cities. Existing local stations would service the feeder trams, enabling passengers from rural areas to access the high-speed line easily. The infrastructure could also be used for local deliveries and freight, which would help get trucks off the road and ease congestion on motorways and in towns and cities.

While Moving Platforms is of course a big idea designed for future implementation, design thinking can equally be applied to small-scale, low-cost solutions to improve transport. Such was the case in Curitiba in Brazil, which developed a simple, clever solution to create one of the most efficient urban rapid transit systems in the world.

In the 1960s, Curitiba city planners feared that population growth would lead to overcrowded development and a sharp increase in car ownership, which in turn would lead to congested roads and air pollution. As a result, they decided to change the face of the city and to invest in mass transit in order to make it the preferred mode of transport in the city. Today, 80 per cent of the population of Curitiba get to and from work through mass transit. The solution was simple. Dedicated lanes for the bus service, pre-boarding fare collection and raised waiting platforms that meant passengers – including those with reduced mobility – would be able to swiftly get on and off the bus.

This was a simple solution, which saw design-thinking radically affect both the quality of the environment, and the experience for passengers. Crucially, local government officials in Curitiba had the foresight and the ambition to think differently and develop a long-term solution. We need more design-thinking at higher level, both in government and in clean tech companies, to ensure that the products and services being developed don't just meet today's needs, but foresee and solve tomorrow's problems.

One of my main inspirations has always been Isambard Kingdom Brunel for his great ambition and vision. Big infrastructure projects rely on a long-term view and sometimes a touch of altruism to affect how we might live in the future. Political terms and short-term investment restrict what can be achieved in the future in order to make quick wins. We need to be thinking about the greater good to truly innovate and progress for subsequent generations.

Paul Priestman is a designer and co-founding director of Priestmangoode, leaders in global travel and transport design. He is also Global Creative Director of CSR Sifang, one of the world's largest rolling stock manufacturers. Priestmangoode works on some of the largest transport and infrastructure projects in the world, from high-speed trains in China to cruise ships and aviation, as well as hospitality and product design. Today, Priestman is known not just for his client work, but for his award-winning future concepts – visionary ideas to improve our everyday lives and encourage sustainable, long-term thinking.

Further details: tel: 020 7935 6665; e-mail: **ideas@priestmangoode.com**; website: **www.priestmangoode.com.**

FIGURE 7.2.2   High-speed trains of the future

Low-carbon mobility

Taking the case of light duty transport, **Liam Lidstone**, transport strategy manager at the Energy Technologies Institute (ETI), argues that economic targets and climate changes goals might be reached without compromising on expectations.

Light vehicles contribute around 16 per cent of UK CO_2 emissions and are a major contributor to congestion and urban air quality. Light vehicles are likely to remain central to UK mobility over the coming decades ahead.

At the ETI, we have researched and analysed the light vehicle market and its energy supply infrastructure to define a potential carbon transition path that is affordable, secure and sustainable for the UK. We found that emissions targets and climate change goals might be reached without consumers needing to compromise on expectations for light vehicles.

Building blocks already in place

The report, which was based on input from academic and industry partners, suggested that many of the fundamental building blocks underpinning a low-carbon mobility future are in development or already in the early stages of commercialization. It found that there are opportunities for UK industry to exploit its existing capabilities in efficiency improvement, electricity systems and in vehicle design and manufacture, in addition to new opportunities in biofuels and energy demand management.

Whilst any low carbon transition will require substantial investment in infrastructure, any large-scale development of a public recharging network is a particularly expensive investment and, according to the report's conclusions, not necessary to meet 2050 targets. Rather, the partial electrification of light-duty vehicles (passenger cars and smaller commercial vehicles) and the roll-out of plug-in hybrids are more realistic and affordable pathways to meet the country's CO_2 targets, providing there is sufficient decarbonization of electricity.

Recommendations looked at what steps to take; what is likely to be the least-risk, lowest-cost route to getting to the solution. As with the government's own light-vehicle ambitions, the report found that fossil fuels, biofuels, powertrain improvements, vehicle electrification (both plug-in and full electric), aerodynamics and light-weighting were all identified as areas which could help the industry reach their economic targets and help meet the necessary climate changes goals without compromising on light-vehicle expectations.

The chicken and the egg

Discussion around the future of low-carbon mobility often comes down to the 'chicken and egg' argument about what comes first – consumer demand or vehicle availability. Consumers won't buy the vehicles unless they are made available; manufacturers won't make them unless they are required to or consumers want to buy them. What's driving reduction in emissions at the moment is largely the regulation that manufacturers are subject to in terms of emissions targets.

As far as consumers are concerned, different types of user have different preferences for vehicles. Some early adopters have shown to be very willing to take up these vehicles. However, our work highlighted that a substantial amount of mainstream consumers aren't willing to pay more for these low-carbon vehicles. People won't pay extra for this option so there needs to be a way of getting those cars to a price point that is acceptable to all buyers.

What's best – charging at home or in the street?

ETI analysis suggests that charging infrastructure should be focused around houses and commercial depots and that a 3-kilowatt charge rate (as opposed to higher power options) would be sufficient for most needs. Whilst a public charging infrastructure might have a supporting role to play in encouraging consumers to purchase hybrid or electric vehicles, our evidence suggests that the actual usage of such charging points is limited.

Borne out by the experience of the government's Plugged-in Places scheme, owners of electric vehicles don't tend to charge at public charging points very often. ETI findings, using travel data, show that with cars, homes are the best location for charging. This is because they are visited more often and left there for longer (predominantly overnight) than any other location. Conveniently this also suits the capabilities of the electricity network, since there is spare capacity overnight.

The view is that the development of low-carbon light vehicles is likely to take place within the existing architecture of vehicles. Building on the existing supply chain and capabilities, to enhance what already exists whilst meeting the ultimate needs of consumers, is a lower-risk, lower-cost route.

In all likelihood a combination of petrol, biofuels and the at-home charging of plug-in hybrid electric vehicles is expected to enable light vehicles to achieve their required contribution to the UK's 2050 energy and climate change goals. Using petrol for light vehicles instead of diesel makes the most efficient overall use of the natural balance of compounds in crude oil and minimizes energy-intensive fuel processing and refining.

There are significant industrial opportunities available to the UK. Firstly through the exploitation of existing UK energy and automotive capabilities in liquid fuels, electricity systems, vehicle design, development and manufacture – and by allowing for the creation of new UK capabilities in the development and exploitation of advanced sustainable biofuels and smart energy demand management.

A need to shift policy

Government policies can help smooth the impact of any transition costs whilst also ensuring that the UK capitalizes on these industrial opportunities. Both the energy and automotive industries are in a position to meet the technology development pathways, but they require a supportive policy environment such that low carbon technology can compete on a level playing field with high-carbon technology.

Developments in other parts of the UK energy infrastructure could have a major effect on the decarbonization of transport and light vehicles. Innovation in other parts of the energy generation system, such as the development of biomass electricity generation with carbon capture and storage could allow some fossil fuel to still be used in light vehicles out to 2050. This could amount to approximately 40 per cent of the current UK light vehicle energy mix, and is likely to significantly reduce the overall cost of carbon reduction.

To download a copy of the insight report or full in-depth report, please visit http://www.eti.co.uk/ldv-an-affordable-transition-to-sustainable-and-secure-energy-from-light-vehicles-in-the-UK. To contact Liam Lidstone, e-mail liam.lidstone@eti.co.uk. (tel: 01509 202 020).

The Energy Technologies Institute (ETI) brings together engineering projects that accelerate the development of affordable, secure and sustainable technologies that help the UK address its long-term emissions reductions targets as well as delivering nearer-term benefits. It is a public/private partnership between global energy and engineering companies – BP, Caterpillar, EDF, E.ON, Rolls-Royce and Shell – and the UK government. Public sector representation is through the Department for Business, Innovation and Skills, with funding channelled through the Technology Strategy Board and the Engineering and Physical Sciences Research Council. The Department of Energy and Climate Change are observers on the Board. Further details: http://eti.co.uk.

LPG Autogas

Rob Shuttleworth, Chief Executive at UKLPG explains the environmental and financial gains of liquefied petroleum gas (LPG) as an alternative fuel.

At present, automotive LPG (liquefied petroleum gas) is the most accessible alternative fuel currently available in the UK and, indeed, worldwide. There are currently more than 16 million vehicles powered by automotive LPG globally and this figure continues to grow year-on-year. Within the UK, the figure stands at around 150,000 vehicles running on LPG and there is a full infrastructure already in place, with more than 1,400 refuelling points, representing more than 10 per cent of forecourts. So, with a national network available, it is ideally situated to reduce vehicle carbon emissions and tackle the growing problem of UK urban air pollution.

With the UK facing a yearly fine of £300 million for failing to meet EU clean air standards, air quality, particularly in urban areas, is a continuing issue. While today's vehicles produce a great deal less pollutants than they used to, they still contribute significantly to air pollution. However, vehicles converted to run on automotive LPG produce far fewer of the harmful emissions associated with traditional fuels and so offer the best environmental alternative.

Based on independent testing of nearly 9,000 cars from the EU that were manufactured recently and that have state-of-the-art pollution controls, those running on automotive LPG produced 11 per cent less CO_2 in operation and about 15 per cent less CO_2 from 'well to wheel', (ie over the entire fuel supply chain) than identical cars that run on petrol. The research[1] also indicates that LPG cars produce less mono-nitrogen oxides (NOx) than both petrol and diesel ones. In fact, when compared to diesel, five times less NOx is emitted. In addition, the testing also highlighted that LPG vehicles produce significantly lower particle emissions when compared to petrol and diesel counterparts.

This can contribute to a significant improvement in local air quality, helping to safeguard public health. In addition, the alternative fuel also produces up to 120 times less of the small particulates found in the tailpipe emissions of some diesel vehicles that are associated with other health hazards, including respiratory problems and developmental difficulties in babies.

According to a report from The Committee on the Medical Effects of Air Pollutants, air pollution in 2008 was responsible for about 29,000 deaths in the UK, which is attributable to long-term exposure to particulate matter, with an average loss of life of 11.5 years. Over 4,250 of these premature deaths occurred in London, where air pollution is the worst in the UK. In addition, nitrogen dioxide (NO_2) also represents a major health risk. A major source of both these dangerous pollutants is diesel exhaust, which the World Health Organization (WHO) has recently classified as a carcinogen.

However, despite the environmental benefits offered by LPG, perhaps the most compelling argument for businesses to adopt the fuel is cost. In fact, when looking at the average fuel prices across the UK, LPG autogas costs around 45 per cent less than unleaded petrol and is even cheaper when compared to diesel. As an example, with a petrol vehicle with an annual mileage of 20,000, an average fuel consumption of 38 miles per gallon and with petrol prices at 131.9 pence, the annual saving that can be made if the vehicle was running on LPG is £1,220.20. When looking at a typical diesel vehicle, the annual savings increase to £1,389.90. In these harsh economic times, an investment in an automotive LPG conversion, by a UKLPG-approved autogas installer, could significantly improve the profitability, as well as the environmental performance of the business fleet.

Despite the benefits that it can offer a business, there remains a slight reticence amongst directors to convert vehicles. One of the main reasons behind this is the perception that conversions are costly and complicated. However, although converting a vehicle to run on automotive LPG does require some work, the vehicle will only be off the road for around three days and a typical conversion would cost around £1,200. Despite the miles per gallon when running on automotive LPG, which is usually around 20 per cent less than petrol, significant savings can be made very quickly across a fleet of vehicles.

The majority of petrol cars currently registered in the UK can be converted to run on LPG autogas. For petrol cars the conversion involves having a second, independent fuel system, including a secondary fuel tank, which is usually fitted in the spare-wheel well, but can sometimes be installed underneath the vehicle. They are available in different sizes, so loss of boot space can be kept to a minimum.

Converting a vehicle to run on LPG autogas is classed as an engine modification and, as such, it is necessary to notify the insurance company. The best way to guarantee insurance is by having the conversion undertaken by a UKLPG-approved autogas installer, (more information can be found at **www.drivelpg. co.uk**). Such accreditation has been designed specifically to demonstrate the mechanic's ability to undertake installations and other related work in a satisfactory manner. This standard also helps to ensure that the fuel remains a safe and reliable part of the future energy landscape for years to come.

In fact, the Autumn Statement that was delivered by the Chancellor of the Exchequer on 5 December 2013 sets out a positive and clear 10-year duty trajectory for automotive LPG and other gaseous fuels. With transparency on the future of the fuel duty, more businesses and fleets are likely to convert their vehicles to run on the fuel, which could have a significant impact on air quality in our urban areas and on the bottom line, especially for companies running high mileage vehicles.

UKLPG continues to lobby for automotive LPG. We want the Chancellor to recognize the importance of industry investment and consumer choice and provide the same level of support as for other road fuel gases. This would encourage responsible motoring and provide financial and environmental benefits to company directors that convert their vehicles to run on this 'green' fuel.

Liquefied petroleum gas (LPG) is a derivative of two large energy industries: natural gas processing and crude oil refining. It is used across the world as a source of energy for heating, cooking and vehicles.

LPG can be transported, stored, and used virtually anywhere in the world. It does not require a fixed network and will not deteriorate over time. It is very clean burning and has lower greenhouse gas emissions than any other fossil fuel when measured on a total fuel cycle.

LPG can be accessible to everyone everywhere today without major infrastructure investment. Nothing needs to be invented and there are enough reserves to last many decades.

LPG is cost-effective, since a high proportion of its energy content is converted into heat and it can be up to five times more efficient than traditional fuels, resulting in less energy wastage and better use of our planet's resources.

LPG is a multi-purpose energy. There are more than a thousand applications, from cooking, heating and transportation, to agricultural grain drying and powering fork lift trucks.

UKLPG is the national trade association and voice of LPG within the UK, representing a membership of companies who are producers, distributors, equipment and service providers and vehicle converters (website: **www.uklpg.org**).

UKLPG's LPG Autogas consumer website – **www.drivelpg.co.uk** – provides a useful calculator for individuals to see what they can save as well as information on conversions and the companies approved to convert vehicles.

For additional information on the Healthy Air Campaign visit: **www.healthyair.org.uk.**

For further information please contact: Lisa Thomson UKLPG, Camden House, Warwick Road, Kenilworth CV8 1TH (tel: 07912 1941001; e-mail: **lisa.thomson@uklpg.org**).

For all press enquiries please contact: Gill Holtom at Prova PR, 7 Church Street, Warwick, Warwickshire CV34 4AB (tel: 01926 776900 or e-mail: **gillh@provapr.co.uk**).

Note

1 Independent research was conducted by Atlantic Consulting – 'A comparative Environmental Impact Assessment of car-and-van fuels'.

INDEX

4Eco 146, 172

Accenture 74
AECOM 148, 149, 152
Ahearn, Mike 42
air pollution
   automotive LPG compared to petrol 231–32
   current priorities for control 199–202
   nitrogen dioxide (NO_2) 199–202, 232
   nitrogen oxides emissions 200–02, 231, 232
   ozone 199
   particulate matter (PM) emissions 199–202, 232
   pollutants in diesel exhaust 232
Air Quality Consultants Ltd 203
American Wind Energy Association 138
antibiotic resistance, and wastewater pollution 193–94
Apple 21
APRES programme 93
Ashberg Ltd 69
Atlantic Supergrid LLP 142
Automotive Council 33
automotive LPG (liquefied petroleum gas) 231–34
automotive sector
   air pollutants in diesel exhaust 232
   CO_2 emissions targets 32–33
   driverless technology 222
   low-carbon vehicles 31–35, 227–30
   potential material cost savings 6, 7
   see also electric vehicles

Barros, Vicente 118
battery technology
   benefits for non-EV applications 218
   developments 213–19
Beaufort Research 158, 163, 165–66
BHP Billiton 68
biodiversity, considerations for major extractive projects 59
bio-electrochemical systems (BES) 189, 195
biofuels, for vehicles 34
biomass 179–84
   feedstock variability 182
   handling and flow systems 179–80
   handling problems 179–82
   key considerations in biomass handling 183–84

methods of processing 179
   solutions for handling problems 182
biomass fuels 16
biomass heat generation, on-site options for businesses 25
Bird & Bird LLP 51, 86
BMW 21
BP 230
brand value, and renewable energy use 21
Branson, Sir Richard 118
BRE consultancy 208, 209
British Gas 42
   Hive application 37
BSkyB 21, 119
BT 119
Buckminster Fuller, Richard 123, 142
building design
   Crossway eco development 171–72
   integrating green technologies 37–40
   passive houses 68
   smart control technologies 37–40
building industry, supply chain management 91–93
buses, initiatives to encourage low carbon vehicles 32, 33
businesses
   carbon measurement 71–75
   energy demand-side management strategies 77–85
   GHG emissions as a material risk 74
   on-site renewable energy generation 21–26
   renewable energy options 24–26
   reporting of GHG emissions 71–75
   role in low carbon transition 21–26
   see also corporate behaviour

Cameron, David 135
capital projects see major capital projects
carbon budgets 95
carbon capture, natural methods 18
carbon capture and storage (CCS) 13, 153–56
   costs and funding 155–56
   projects update 153–55
   role in mitigating climate change 153
Carbon Capture & Storage Association (CCSA) 156
carbon dioxide (CO_2) emissions
   automotive LPG compared to petrol 231
   developments in light vehicles 227–28

Carbon Disclosure Project (CDP)   47–49
    as GHG reporting driver   71–74
carbon footprinting   72
carbon measurement
    CDP as reporting driver   71–74
    GHG emissions as a material risk   74
    in businesses   71–75
    third-party assurance on reporting   73, 74
Carbon Plans (UK)   32
carbon reduction, challenges of decarbonization
        15–19
Carbon Reduction Commitment (CRC) energy
        efficiency scheme   48
cassiterite, sourcing issues   90, 93
Caterpillar   230
Centre for Alternative Technology   19
Chase, Robin   42
Chung, Andrew   42
circular economy   3–8, 205–08
    adopting circular thinking   208
    as driver of innovation   7
    benefits for land productivity   7–8
    changing business models   207
    definition   205
    designing for resource efficiency   206–07
    designing out waste   4–5
    economic resilience produced by   8
    future developments   208
    job creation potential   7
    potential economic benefits   6
    potential net material cost savings   6–7
    potential value in the waste stream   206
    problem of resource scarcity and waste
        205–06
    product collection and reuse   207
    role of renewable energy   5
    sources of value creation   5–6
    system changes required   207–08
    trends towards   8
    users instead of consumers   5
CleanWeb Factory Ltd   44, 120
climate change
    challenges of decarbonization   15–19
    costs of   15
    global energy efficiency challenge   118
    policy initiatives for mitigation   32–33
    pressure to address   21
    role of carbon capture and storage (CCS)   153
    Zero Carbon Britain strategy   15–19
Climate Change Act (UK, 2008)   32
coltan, sourcing issues   90, 93
combined heat and power (CHP) systems, options
        for businesses   25–26
Committee on Climate Change (UK)   32, 95
compressed natural gas (CNG) fuel for vehicles
        34
Confederation of British Industry (CBI)   41

construction industry, supply chain management
        91–93
consumers
    approval of companies which reduce GHG
        emissions   75
    awareness of sustainability issues   68
    changing energy use patterns   111–13
    energy demand-side management strategies
        77–85
    motivations for reducing energy consumption
        118–19
    response to increasing household energy bills
        68
    shift in transport preferences   221–22
    transition to users   5
copyright   102
corporate behaviour
    consideration of community and environmental
        impacts   46–47
    disclosure of environmental emissions   47–49
    energy demand-side management   50
    factors influencing boardroom decisions   45–51
    greening the supply chain   49
    on-site renewable energy generation   49–50
    sustainability strategies   45–51
    see also businesses
corporate social responsibility, supply chain
        management   89–94
Crossrail   93
Crossway eco development   171–72
CSR Sifang   222, 225
Czisch, Gregor   124, 126

Defence industry, benefits from battery technology
        218
demand-side management   77–85
    financial considerations   83–85
    managing the process   80
    ownership of assets   80–83
    range of possible solutions   78–80
    role of the energy services company   77–78
demand-side response   78–79
Democratic Republic of Congo (DRC)   90, 93
Department for Business, Innovation and
        Skills (UK)   230
Department for Energy and Climate Change (UK)
        95, 230
Desertec   124, 125, 136
Deutsche Bank   73
diesel exhaust, air pollutants in   232
Dow Chemical, reputation case study   91
driverless technology   222

eco developments   171–72
economic models
    circular economy concept   3–8, 205–08
    linear model of consumption   3–4

EDF   12, 230
Edison, Thomas   138
electric vehicles   31–35, 212–19
    battery improvements benefit other applications
        218
    battery safety issue   213–14, 215
    battery technology   213–19
    charging at home or in the street   228–29
    electricity requirements   13
    energy demands   112
    environmental impact of the Li-S battery   216
    factors constraining uptake   213–14
    first commercially available vehicle with Li-S
        battery   217
    history of development   214
    Induct Navia electric vehicle   217
    lithium air battery   219
    lithium sulfur (Li-S) battery   214–18, 219
    performance of the Li-S battery   215–16
    range anxiety issue   213
    requirements for mass-market adoption   217
    see also low-carbon light vehicles; low carbon
        vehicles
electricity distribution
    innovation in   113–15
    new demands on electricity networks
        109–16
    smart grids   117–18
    supergrid concept   123–42
electricity grids
    AC and DC compared   131–32, 138–40
    alternatives to the supergrid   141–42
    bolstering existing AC grids   136–41
    changes caused by renewables   128
    economic drivers for interconnectors
        (interties)   131
    effects of fluctuating demand on cost   127
    emergence of a supergrid   128–36
    high-voltage direct current (HVDC) links
        128–32
    how they make electricity cheaper   128
    improved long-distance transmission technology
        131–32
    laying an HVDC cable   140–41
    National Grid   49, 127, 147
electricity market reform (EMR) in the UK
        155–56
Ellen MacArthur Foundation   9, 206
Elliott, David   169–70
energy consumption in the UK (2007–2012)
        43–44
energy cost   22
energy efficiency
    investment in   41–43
    levels of waste in the UK   43
    potential benefits   41
    smart energy   117–20

energy generation
    decentralized generation   67–69, 78–79
    distributed generation   13
    innovation in response to new demands
        110–11
energy informatics   see informatics
energy infrastructure, transformation of   13
energy innovation   11–14
    support for new technologies   13–14
Energy Innovation Centre   116
energy markets, modelling   97
energy performance contracts   78–79
Energy Savings Trust   41
energy services companies, demand-side
        management for consumers   77–85
energy sources, range and diversity   110–11
energy supply security, reducing risks   22–23
energy sustainability   22
energy system modelling   95–98
    assessment of major investment options   98
    characteristics of energy systems   96–97
    insights into energy markets   97
    uses and limitations   96
Energy Technologies Institute (ETI)   95, 99,
        227–29, 230
energy trilemma concept   22–23
energy usage monitoring   11
energy use, response to changing patterns and
        demands   111–13
Engineering and Physical Sciences Research Council
        230
environmental emissions, requirement for
        companies to disclose   47–49
environmental impacts, and the triple bottom
        line   87–89
Environmental Resources Management (ERM)
        61
E.ON   230
ERM Certification and Verification Services
        (ERM CVS)   75
ESME (Energy System Modelling Environment)
        tool   95–96
European energy supergrid   124, 126, 128–36
European Union
    support for a supergrid   130, 135, 136
    support for ocean energy technologies
        160–61, 163
extractives sector
    biodiversity considerations   59
    capital project design for the future   58
    causes of delays in major capital projects
        53–58
    clean tech blueprint   58–60
    considerations related to water   59
    energy sources   59
    flagship extractive projects   60–61
    innovation in project development   58–60

issues related to waste   59
non-technical causes of delays   53–58
non-technical risk assessment   60
role of IT in major project development   60
transport considerations   60

Facebook   21, 119
fast moving consumer goods, potential material
    cost savings   7
flexible energy supply contracts   78–80
flue gas, energy produced from   190, 192
food production, reducing impacts of   16–17
food waste in the UK   43
Ford
    EcoBoost engines   31
    investment in low-emission technology   33
Formula One, energy efficiency innovations   41
fossil fuels, future role of   13, 68–69
Friends of the Supergrid   133, 136
funding innovative energy technologies   13–14
    challenges for investors   65–69
    changing business model of utilities   67–69
    decentralized generation of energy   67–69
    insurance for projects   67
    public funding support   67
    venture funds   65–69

gaseous fuels, for vehicles   34
Gates, Bill   118
General Electric (GE)   45, 50
Google   11, 45
    acquisition of Nest   37
    renewable energy generation   49
Green Bus Funds   32, 33
Green Investment Bank (GIB)   42–43
greenhouse gas (GHG) emissions
    as a material risk for investors   74
    CDP as reporting driver   71–74
    consumer awareness   75
    in a zero carbon Britain   17
    involving the supply chain   74
    reporting by businesses   71–75
    requirement for companies to disclose   47–49
    third-party assurance on reporting   73, 74
    UK targets   15
Greenpeace   49

Hawkes, Richard   171–72
healthcare devices   38
Healthy Air Campaign   234
heat pumps, domestic   13
Heatmiser   38
high-voltage direct current (HVDC) links   128–32
    laying an HVDC cable   140–41
Honda   21
hospital wastewater treatment   193–94

hybrid vehicles   31–35
hydrogen, as a fuel and storage medium   11–12
hydropower, pumped storage hydropower (PSH)
    schemes   147–52

IBM Battery 500 project   219
ICT, smart energy   117–20
immerSUN microgeneration controller   144–45,
    172
Induct Navia electric vehicle   217
informatics
    energy informatics   44
    smart energy   117–20
    super-useful information   119–20
innovation
    energy innovation   11–14
    in the circular economy   7
    intellectual property (IP) protection   101–06
    support for new technologies   13–14
intellectual property (IP)
    as a business asset   102–03
    dealing with third-party IP rights   105
    management of   104–05
    patents to protect technical innovations
        102, 103–06
    protection for innovation   101–06
    protection strategies   104
    recycling old IP   106
    types of IP rights   102
internet of things   37
iPad-based control systems   38
Irish-Scottish Links on Energy Study (ISLES)   136
ISO 14001   74

Jaguar   49
    investment in low-emission technology   33
job creation, in the circular economy   7

Kahn, Herman   173
Kayser, Ottmar   73
KSR Architects   40

L'Oreal   49
land degradation, costs of   7–8
Land Rover, investment in low-emission technology
    33
light vehicles   see low-carbon light vehicles
linear model of production and
    consumption   3–4
liquefied petroleum gas (LPG)   see LPG
liquid natural gas (LNG) fuel for vehicles   34
lithium air battery   219
lithium sulfur (Li-S) battery   214–18, 219
low-carbon light vehicles   227–30
    building blocks already in place   227–28
    charging at home or in the street   228–29

hybrid vehicles   228
industrial opportunities for the UK   229
meeting buyers' requirements   228
meeting emissions targets   227–28
need for a shift in government policy   229–30
vehicle availability   228
low-carbon transition, role of businesses   21–26
Low Carbon Vehicle Partnership (LowCVP)   33, 35
low-carbon vehicles
cost efficiency   34
market   31
policy initiatives   32–33
technology options   34
LPG (liquefied petroleum gas)
features of   233–34
range of applications   233–34
sources of   233–34
LPG (liquefied petroleum gas) autogas   34, 231–34
converting vehicles to run on   232–33
cost effectiveness   232, 234
emissions compared to petrol   231–32
UK network of refuelling points   231

machinery and equipment, potential material
cost savings   6, 7
major capital projects
biodiversity considerations   59
causes of delays   53–58
clean tech blueprint   58–60
considerations related to water   59
design for the future   58
energy sources   59
flagship extractive projects   60–61
innovation in project development   58–60
issues related to waste   59
non-technical risk assessment   60
non-technical risk factors   53–58
role of IT in project development   60
transport considerations   60
MARINET   163, 165
Markal energy system modelling tool   95
Marks & Spencer   119
mass transit solutions   222–24
materials handling, biomass fuels   179–84
Materials Handling Engineers Association   184
McKinsey & Company   6–7, 206
mechanical and electrical (M&E) components,
responsible sourcing   92–93
Medgrid   136
methanol, as fuel for vehicles   34
Mewburn Ellis LLP   106
Microsoft   45
mining   see extractives sector
mobile phone companies, sourcing of coltan
and cassiterite   90, 93
modelling   see energy systems modelling

Narec Capital   69
National Grid   49, 127, 147
National Renewable Energy Centre (Narec)
69, 163
Nike, reputation case study   90
Nike, Fuelband   38
Nissan
electric battery Leaf model   31
investment in low-emission technology   33
nitrogen, recovery from wastewater   194–95
nitrogen dioxide (NO_2) air pollution   199–202,
232
nitrogen oxides emissions   200–02, 231, 232
North Sea Countries Offshore Grid Initiative   136
nuclear power   12
plant decommissioning costs   177

O'Connor, Eddie   136
ocean energy   see tidal energy technologies;
wave energy technologies
offshore wind farms   173–77
offshore wind power, cost of   12
off-site renewable power purchase agreements
78–79
oil and gas   see extractives sector
OpenTRV   42
OXIS Energy Ltd   212, 216, 217, 218, 219

particulate matter (PM) emissions
air pollution control   199–202
from automotive LPG   232
patents, to protect technical innovations
102, 103–06
pharmaceutical pollution of wastewater   193–94
Philips   38
phosphorus, recovery from wastewater   195–97
plug-in vehicle programme   32, 34
Plugged-in Places scheme   229
Priestmangoode   221, 222–25
Primark, reputation case study   90, 92
public funding, support for innovative energy
technologies   67
public transport   222–25
pumped storage hydropower (PSH) schemes
147–52

rail transport   222–24, 225
Redstack   190
Refuse-Derived Fuel (RDF)   179
registered designs   102
registered trademarks   102
Reicher, Dan   42
renewable energy
competitive pricing   12
cost problem   132–33
effects on electricity grids   128

harnessing the power of the planet   124
indigenous sources in Britain   18
intermittency problem   133
investment payback period   22
offshore wind farms   173–77
off-site power purchase agreements   78–79
on-site generation by businesses   21–26,
    49–50
options for powering business   24–26
potential benefits of a supergrid   132–34,
    136–37
prospects for self-generation   143–46
pumped storage hydropower (PSH) schemes
    147–52
role in the circular economy   5
self-consumption technologies   144–46
solar technology   169–72
tidal energy technologies   159–65
wave energy technologies   159–65
RenewableUK   174, 178
reputational risks
    case studies   90–91
    social considerations   89–94
RES (Renewable Energy Systems)   20, 27
resource efficiency   see circular economy
resources
    increasing cost of   4
    potential cost savings in the circular economy
        6–7
    price volatility   4, 7
    supply disruptions   4, 7
    value creation in the circular economy   5–6
Responsible Solutions Ltd   88, 94
responsible sourcing   87–94
reverse cycle activities   8
reversed electro-dialysis (RED)   190, 191
Revolutionary Electric Vehicle Battery project
    217
Rolls-Royce   230

Sainsbury   48
salinity gradient energy   189–90, 191
Samsung   176
Scottish Informatics and Computer Science
    Alliance   117
self-consumption technologies   144–46
self-generation of renewable energy   143–46
Senvion   176
Shell   230
Siemens   176
smart cities   37–38
smart energy systems   13, 117–20
smart grids   117–20
smart meters   11, 117–20
smart phone-based control systems   38

SMC (building services consultant)   39, 40
solar photovoltaic (PV) systems   170–71
    on-site options for businesses   24–25
solar technology   169–72
    current state of development   169–70
    development and innovation   12
    energy storage battery improvements   218
    expectations for the future   172
    history of development   170
    in eco developments   171–72
    types of   170–71
solar thermal systems   171
Sony, Lifelog products   38
sourcing responsibly   87–94
special areas of conservation (SACs)   202
STOR (short-term operating reserve)   147
storage of energy
    battery technology developments   213–19
    pumped storage hydropower (PSH) schemes
        147–52
supergrid concept   123–42
    AC and DC compared   131–32, 138–40
    bolstering existing AC grids   136–41
    economic drivers for interconnectors (interties)
        131
    emergence of a supergrid   128–36
    European energy supergrid   124, 126,
        128–36
    harnessing the power of the planet   124
    help with renewable energy problems
        132–34, 136–37
    improved long-distance transmission
        technology   131–32
    laying an HVDC cable   140–41
    projects in development   134–35
    stimulus of public policy   130
    supporters and proponents   135–36
    viability of alternatives   141–42
super-useful information, and consumer behaviour
    119–20
supply chain management
    and the CDP report   49
    construction industry   91–93
    corporate social responsibility   89–94
    reducing GHG emissions   74
    reputational risks   89–94
    responsible sourcing   87–94
sustainability
    corporate strategies   45–51
    of energy supply   22
    responsible sourcing   87–94

Technology Strategy Board   13–14, 230
Tesco   43, 48, 73, 119
Tesla, Nikola   138

tidal energy technologies   12, 159–65
    certified standards approach   163–65
    de-risking the industry   163–65
    issues facing the industry   161–62
    potential supply of ocean energy   159–60
    role of government   160–61, 162
    technical and non-technical barriers   161–62
    technologies in development   160–61
Toyota
    hybrid Auris model   31
    investment in low-emission technology   33
transport
    considerations for major extractive projects
        60
    sustainable strategy for the UK   31–35
    see also automotive sector; electric vehicles;
        low-carbon light vehicles; low-carbon vehicles
transport design   221–25
    driverless technology   222
    mass transit solutions   222–24
    Moving Platforms concept   222–24
    public transport   222–25
    rail transport   222–24, 225
    shift in consumer behaviour   221–22
triple bottom line   87–94
    corporate social responsibility   89–94
    environmental impacts   87–89

UKLPG   233, 234
utility companies
    challenge of delivering smart energy   119–20
    changing business model   67–69

value creation, in the circular economy   5–6
ValuefromUrine project   189, 195
venture funds, funding innovative energy
        technologies   65–69
Vestas/Mitsubishi   176
Virgin Media   119

Walmart   21, 49
waste
    elimination in the circular economy   4–5
    food waste in the UK   43

issues for major extractive projects   59
    materials recovery and reuse   4–5
wastewater treatment
    nutrient control and recovery   194–97
    pharmaceutical pollution   193–94
water, issues for major extractive projects   59
water footprinting   72
water technologies
    bio-electrochemical systems (BES)   189, 195
    challenges of the water-energy-food nexus
        187–88
    control of antibiotic pollution   193–94
    de-ammonification processes   195
    energy from water   188–92
    nutrient control and recovery   194–97
    pumped storage hydropower (PSH) schemes
        147–52
    reversed electro-dialysis (RED)   190, 191
    salinity gradient energy   189–90, 191
    wastewater treatment processes   193–97
    see also tidal energy technologies;
        wave energy technologies
WaterCampus Leeuwarden   198
wave energy technologies   12, 159–65
    certified standards approach   163–65
    de-risking the industry   163–65
    issues facing the industry   161–62
    potential supply of ocean energy   159–60
    role of government   160–61, 162
    technical and non-technical barriers
        161–62
    technologies in development   160–61
Westinghouse, George   138
Wetsus   188, 190, 194, 195, 197–98
wind power
    cost of offshore energy production   12
    offshore wind farms   173–77
    on- and off-site options for businesses   24
wisdom hierarchy   119–20
The Wolfson Centre for Bulk Solids Handling
        Technology   181, 184
World Energy Council   21

Zero Carbon Britain strategy   15–19

INDEX OF ADVERTISERS

Aecom	148
Beaufort	158
Bird & Bird	ii
Corvus	iii
Oxis	212
Renewable UK	174
RES	20
Responsible Solutions	88